D0200838

HOPE FOR

TROUBLED HEARTS

FAILING MARRIAGES

THOSE WHO LOST LOVED ONES

SINGLE PEOPLE

THOSE WHO GRIEVE

PRODIGAL CHILDREN

THOSE FACING CRISIS

HOPE FOR

TROUBLED HEARTS

THOSE WHO LOST LOVED ONES

SINGLE PEOPLE

THOSE WHO GRIEVE

PRODIGAL CHILDREN

FAILING MARRIAGES

THOSE FACING CRISIS

GREG LAURIE

International Standard Book Number: 978-1-61291-315-5

Published by Kerygma Publishing

Cover design by Ross Geerdes

Coordination: FM Management, Ltd.

Contact: mgf@fmmgt.net

Unless otherwise indicated, all Scripture quotations are taken from: *The Holy Bible*, New King James Version © 1984 by Thomas Nelson, Inc.

Scripture quotations marked (NIV) are from *The Holy Bible*, New International Version®, NIV®. Copyright © 1973, 1978, 1984 by Biblica. Used by permission of Zondervan Publishing House.

Scripture quotations marked (NLT) are taken from The New Living Translation, copyright © 1996, 2004, 2007 by Tyndale House Foundation. Used by permission of Tyndale House Publishers Inc., Carol Stream, Illinois 60188. All rights reserved.

Scripture quotations marked (TLB) are taken from The Living Bible, copyright © 1971 by Tyndale House Publishers, Wheaton, Illinois.

Scripture quotations marked (MSG) are taken from *THE MESSAGE*, by Eugene Peterson. Copyright © 1993, 1994, 1995, 1996, 2000, 2001, 2002. Used by permission of NavPress Publishing Group. All rights reserved.

Scripture quotations marked (PH) are from The New Testament in Modern English, Revised Edition © 1958, 1960, 1972 by J. B. Phillips.

Printed in the United States of America

1 2 3 4 5 6 7 8 / 17 16 15 14 13 12

CONTENTS

HOPE FOR
TROUBLED HEARTS
THOSE WHO LOST LOVED ONES
THOSE WHO
GRIEVE
THOSE FACING CRISIS
FAILING MARRIAGES

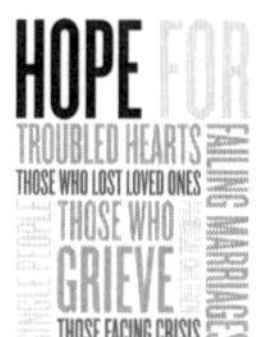

INTRODUCTION

AS I WRITE THESE words, I'm looking at an old snapshot of myself as a child, standing close beside my beautiful mother—who more than anything else wanted to look like Marilyn Monroe.

As I look into my own face, I see discomfort and unhappiness, although I don't remember why I felt that way at the time.

But I can guess.

As far back as I can remember, my mother never hugged me or told me she loved me. In the picture, she was all dressed up and probably on her way out somewhere, and I didn't know when I would see her again.

The picture was taken at my grandparents' house, where I spent most of my time. My mother would occasionally make a surprise appearance, and I would be so excited to see her. And then she would disappear again, maybe for days, maybe for weeks. This was the cycle of my life growing up: being with her, not being with her, and dealing with all of the trials she went through as an alcoholic and someone who was married and divorced seven times.

As a young teenager, I was sent to military school: the Southern California Military Academy, up on Signal Hill in Long Beach. (It's no longer there.) I spent some lonely years there, though as I look back, I would have to say that was probably one of the more stable times of my life.

At the academy, it was mandatory to attend chapel every Sunday, so along with the other cadets, I would sit in chapel services each week. To this day, I remember a song we used to sing: "You'll Never Walk Alone." It began, "When you walk through a storm, hold your head up high . . ." and went on to speak about the end of the storm, a golden sky, and walking with a hope-filled heart, knowing that "you'll never walk alone."

For some reason, that song resonated with me. Despite the turmoil of my upbringing, I had an optimistic feeling that somehow, some way, things were going to get better for me. I always believed there was a God. I always believed in Jesus Christ, or at least in as much as I knew about Him.

When I lived in my grandparents' home, they had one of those classic portraits of Jesus hanging on the wall. As a little boy, I would look at this depiction of Jesus, sort of gazing off somewhere, and a feeling of great admiration for Him rose up in my heart. I remember thinking to myself, *I wish I could know this Jesus. But He came. He died. He's gone now—or maybe up there somewhere, but I don't know where. And I don't know how to communicate with Him.*

Though my life took any number of difficult twists and turns through those childhood and teen years, in 1970 I heard a message on my high school campus about Jesus Christ that I understood. As a result, I prayed and asked

Christ to come into my life.

That is when my childhood optimism found its true Object.

That is when things started turning out for the better.

And that is when I found real, solid hope for the first time in my life.

Life still has its twists and turns, its moments of great joy as well as deep sorrow. But through all the ups and downs, that hope I found in 1970 has sustained me through the dark times and has given me peace and confidence at all times.

I hope that the following pages will bring that same encouragement to your heart, no matter what your present situation.

CHAPTER ONE

HOPE FOR THOSE FACING CRISIS

IT'S A DAY LIKE any other day. You get out of bed, take a shower, eat breakfast, brush your teeth, and read your Bible and pray, committing your day to the Lord. In other words, you're just walking through the normal routine of your morning.

And then it happens—out of the clear blue sky, as they say.

You get a call from a police officer or friend telling you there has been a terrible accident. Your doctor rings your cell; he needs to see you immediately because of something he found in a recent medical test. You find a note on the counter from your spouse, flatly stating that he or she is done with the marriage. Or maybe you get to work and find that dreaded pink slip waiting on your desk.

Crisis, when it comes, hits hard and fast. Pain knocks on your front door, shoulders its way inside, takes up residence without your permission, and refuses to be evicted.

You wouldn't wish what is happening to you on your worst enemy. Nevertheless, it is reality in your life. One way or another, you will have to walk through it.

For Job, it was when his whole world came crashing down on his head in a matter of hours. For young Joseph, it was when his own brothers betrayed him and sold him as a slave. For Jesus, it was when one of His own handpicked disciples turned on Him.

For you, it might be something else.

A strong and unexpected storm has overtaken your little boat, utterly overwhelming you and swamping you. You find yourself wondering, *Will I even survive this? Will I make it through this alive? Is there any hope for me?*

Let's read a familiar passage of Scripture together as we consider this matter of facing crises in our lives:

> When He got into a boat, His disciples followed Him. And suddenly a great tempest arose on the sea, so that the boat was covered with the waves. But He was asleep. Then His disciples came to Him and awoke Him, saying, "Lord, save us! We are perishing!"
>
> But He said to them, "Why are you fearful, O you of little faith?" Then He arose and rebuked the winds and the sea, and there was a great calm. So the men marveled, saying, "Who can this be, that even the winds and the sea obey Him?" (Matthew 8:23-27)

WHAT CAN WE LEARN FROM THIS STORY?

1. Storms will come into our lives.

The tempest that hit the Sea of Galilee that day was a serious one. In the original language, the word used for *storm* in this story is elsewhere translated "earthquake." The squall that hit that little fishing boat was so severe that waves were breaking over the boat, filling it up.

Some of these disciples were seasoned sailors and had grown up around the Sea of Galilee. Storms were nothing new to them. But this squall came up so quickly and turned so violent that they cried out in fear for their lives.

It's the way most of us react when we're hit with a sudden storm. We say things like, "Why is this happening to me?" Or, "What have I done to deserve this?"

The fact is, we may never get answers to questions like that. It's very unlikely we will ever have the answers to the "whys" of life until we get to heaven.

Jesus made no attempt to explain why His disciples had found themselves in a terrifying and life-threatening situation. What concerned Him much more was how they *dealt* with the crisis when it hit.

That's a good model for us as well. Instead of pouring our emotional energy into asking why, we could do better asking questions like "How should I respond?" or "What should I do in times like these?"

My simple objective in this chapter is to bring hope to you and to encourage you not to give up in the face of your crisis—whether it is minor or threatens to overwhelm you. In fact, I want to show you how the very crisis you are enduring right now might turn out to be one of the greatest blessings in your life.

Somewhere along the way, we may have picked up the false notion that Christians ought to be exempt from suffering or that tragedies only happen to others: *Someone else will face a divorce, but not me. Someone else will get a diagnosis of cancer, but not me. Someone else will be seriously injured in a car wreck, but not me. Someone else will have problems with their kids, but not me.*

If that is what you've been telling yourself, then it is time you woke up and smelled the coffee. It really doesn't matter how much you love the Lord or how much the Lord loves you, you are not exempt from crisis or tragedy or heartache. Sooner or later, your life will be touched by these things. The storm will come, and the Lord will be watching to see how you respond.

After our son died in a car accident in 2008, I remember someone saying to me, "Why has this happened to you *of all people*?" I found that to be a curious question.

Why Greg Laurie?

Why *not* Greg Laurie?

Am I supposed to get a free pass because I'm a preacher? No, the fact is that I live in the same fallen world as you do. And the Bible says that the rain falls upon the just and the unjust (see Matthew 5:45).

It's a mistake to always be looking for a cause and effect for everything that happens to us. Sometimes we will look at someone else's life and say, "They did such and such, and look what happened to them!" Maybe that's true, and maybe it isn't. The fact is, we might be reading it all wrong; sometimes bad stuff just happens, and there is no cause and effect at all. Tragedy happens simply because we live in a sinful, fallen world—and for no other discernible reason. We have to face sin and sickness and aging and disabilities and death in this life, even though none of those things were part of God's original plan.

On one occasion, the disciples brought up the subject

of a tower that had fallen on a group of Gentiles, killing eighteen of them. Were the eighteen the worst sinners in Jerusalem because this happened to them? Did they fall under God's judgment because they were Gentile pagans and not good Jews?

Jesus surprised them with His answer: "I tell you, no! But unless you repent, you too will all perish" (Luke 13:5, NIV). I think the Lord was saying that bad things happen inexplicably, and we need to be ready.

In the book of Job, bad things happened to a man, not because he was ungodly or godless but because he was godly. What did Job do wrong to have such terrible things befall him in the course of a single day? When you read the first chapter of his book, it talks about what a wonderful man of God he was—how he prayed for his family, how he cared for them. This guy was so right on that God actually was bragging on him, saying to the angels (with Satan among them), "Have you considered My servant Job, that there is none like him on the earth, a blameless and upright man, one who fears God and shuns evil?" (Job 1:8). Yet in a single day, Job lost just about everything that had mattered to him—including his children, his possessions, his servants, his reputation, and his health. So let's just leave those mysteries in the hands of God. We don't know the whys. But we do know this: God has a plan, and His plan is good.

Randy Alcorn wrote,

> If we come to see the purpose of the universe as God's long-term glory rather than our short-term happiness, then we will undergo a critical paradigm shift in tackling the problem of evil and suffering. The world has

> gone terribly wrong. God is going to fix it. First, for His eternal glory. Second, for our eternal good.[1]

That's a different way of thinking for most of us, isn't it? We tend to think of the world revolving around us: We're the star of our own film, the featured character of our own novel. But then tragedy crashes into our lives, and we're blown away by it. *What is this? This makes no sense! Why is this happening to me?*

But wait a second. The big picture in life is ultimately about God's glory, not about our personal happiness.

And here is a fact we have difficulty accepting at first: Our hope actually will grow through times of hardship and adversity in our lives.

The Bible tells us,

> We can rejoice, too, when we run into problems and trials, for we know that they help us develop endurance. And endurance develops strength of character, and character strengthens our confident hope of salvation. And this hope will not lead to disappointment. For we know how dearly God loves us, because he has given us the Holy Spirit to fill our hearts with his love. (Romans 5:3-5, NLT)

Wait a minute. Could that be right? Did Paul just use the words *trials* and *problems* in the same paragraph where he speaks of God's love for us? How could that be? If God loved me, wouldn't He *remove* the trials and the problems?

The fact is, He might. But maybe He won't. That is up to God.

So . . . back to our story. Here are the disciples in this radical storm, fearing for their very lives, with waves actually cresting over the top of the boat. And Jesus, their Master and Lord, is sound asleep.

I have seen a boat very similar to the vessel these guys would have been in. If you go to Israel today, there is a little museum that houses what they call "the Jesus boats." And the archaeologists have found and identified a fishing boat that is probably very similar to what fishermen would have been using in the first century.

It's a simple little boat, not very big, and not very sophisticated. Jesus managed to go to sleep underneath the top deck. It would have been wet and cold in that storm, but He seemed to be exhausted after a hard day of ministry.

Have you ever felt like Jesus was asleep when you were calling on Him? *Lord, where are You? Are You paying attention? Do You see what trouble I'm in?* In a technical sense, Jesus the God-Man was asleep that day. But in a broader sense, God never sleeps. We are told in Psalm 121:4, "He who watches over Israel will neither slumber nor sleep" (NIV).

Jesus was asleep because He was resting confidently in the will of His Father—and the disciples should have done that, too. He had told them they would be fine. In Mark's version of this same story, Jesus said, "Let us cross over to the other side" (Mark 4:35). And that meant they certainly would get there. He didn't promise them an easy trip, but He promised them a safe arrival. They might have rested in that assurance, but panic took over instead and they hurried to wake Him up.

2. We need to cry out to Jesus in the midst of our storm.

They yelled, "Lord save us! We are perishing!" (Matthew 8:25).

Oh no! We're all gonna die!

The shrieking winds and crashing waves didn't wake Jesus, but the cry of His people did. The moment His children cried out, He responded immediately and powerfully.

People often will cry out to God in times of great crisis. Some say there are no atheists in foxholes, but I'm sure there are. Scared atheists or despairing atheists maybe, but atheists all the same. The Bible tells us, "The fool has said in his heart, 'There is no God' " (Psalm 14:1). And that foolishness can persist, even in a life-threatening crisis. Nevertheless, in times of great difficulty or danger, many people will cry out to God.

The story is told of a hardened old sea captain who was very vocal about his atheism. And then one night, during a violent storm, he was washed overboard, and his men actually heard him crying out to God for help. When they finally rescued him, one of the men asked, "Didn't you say that you didn't believe in God?"

The old captain answered, "Well, if there isn't a God, there *ought to be* in times like this."

So then, even nonbelievers can cry out to God. But in that storm on Galilee, it was the Lord's own who were calling out to Him. The fact is, the Lord will sometimes let us hit bottom so that we will finally recognize our need for Him. Thomas Watson said, "When God lays men on their backs, then they look up to heaven."

By the way, we should never think of prayer as a last resort, but rather a *first* resort. If you are injured or ill, by all means get yourself to a doctor. If you are threatened, call the police. Those are logical, practical steps to take. But the first thing you should do is pray, even if all you have time for is a quick cry to God for help. *Lord, please help me. Lord, intervene in this. Lord, show me what to do. Lord, give me wisdom.*

Sometimes people will do everything they can to fix their situation, and then when nothing has worked, they will say, "All we can do now is just . . . (gulp) pray."

(All they can do now is call on the almighty God, the Creator of the heavens and the earth? Isn't that too bad?)

Cry out to the Lord. If you are ill, ask God for His healing touch. I don't care what the doctors have said. I don't care if they have told you there is only a 10 percent chance of survival. You're talking to the all-powerful Sovereign of the universe. As the prophet said, "Surely the arm of the LORD is not too short to save, nor his ear too dull to hear" (Isaiah 59:1, NIV).

Call out to the Lord, and put your trust in Him. No matter what your situation might be, God is still in the miracle business. And remember, if you know someone who is sick or struggling with some disease, they need *hope*, not doomsday talk!

Just recently I was talking to two men, and one of them revealed that he had a particular kind of cancer. "Oh yeah?" the other said. "My uncle died of that same cancer."

I wanted to smack that guy! What a time to run off at the mouth! That person was well aware he could die from his condition. What he needed in that moment were words of hope, not some stupid remark that doesn't help anyone. Let's emphasize hope whenever we can. If you can't say anything else, assure that individual of your prayers. Or say nothing at all! Just don't blurt out the first thing that comes into your mind.

So the Lord's men cried out to Him for help, and He

came up on deck. In an instant, He had stopped that storm in its tracks: "He arose and rebuked the winds and the sea, and there was a great calm" (Matthew 8:26).

They had cried out to Jesus, and He immediately intervened. Sometimes, He will do just that. He will hear your cry and step in to remove the thing that frightens or troubles you. Call out to Him, and don't hesitate!

3. God has His purposes in the storms of life.

Remember this: No matter what, God is in control and has a plan.

So we look to the Lord in our crisis, recognizing that He can accomplish great things in and through our hardships, disappointments, and setbacks. Why? Because God knows all things, past, present, and future, He is uniquely qualified to know when to ordain or permit evil and suffering, and when not to. Therefore, if the Lord allows something to enter your life, He has a plan in mind for dealing with it.

We love to follow the Lord when things are going along the way we want them to. That's just human nature. I was playing with my granddaughters the other day, and they were so excited and having so much fun. There were toys all over, and it looked like a whirlwind had ripped through the room.

Then I said, "Now it's time to clean up."And suddenly it wasn't fun anymore.

"I *always* have to clean up," said one.

"Yeah, I do, too," said the other.

I said, "Come on now, girls. We took this stuff out to play with it, and now we get to put it away."

The girls weren't happy. They weren't happy with me, and they weren't happy with the situation.

In the same way, we get excited when the Lord opens a door of opportunity, and we tell Him, "Oh Lord, I love following You. It's so exciting to be a Christian and to be in Your will."

But then we hit a rough patch, and we say, "Hey, this isn't fun anymore. I don't like this. This *hurts*. I don't want to go through this. Take it away!"

I like the attitude that David had in Psalm 23. He begins like this:

> The Lord is my shepherd;
> I shall not want.
> He makes me to lie down in green pastures;
> He leads me beside the still waters.
> He restores my soul;
> He leads me in the paths of righteousness
> For His name's sake. (verses 1-3)

It sounds like he's saying, "Man, life is *good*." But then He says,

> Yea, though I walk through the valley of the shadow of death,
> I will fear no evil;
> For You are with me;
> Your rod and Your staff, they comfort me.
> You prepare a table before me in the presence of my enemies. (verses 4-5)

What? Darkness? Enemies? We love those green pastures, still waters, and paths of righteousness. But we aren't really excited about a valley—especially when the shadow of death is written over it. We appreciate His preparing a table for us, but does it have to be in the presence of people who hate us? Nevertheless, He is with us in those times as well. That's what it is to follow the Lord.

We trust Him in the sunlight and soft winds as well as in the nights and storms.

BUT WHY DOES HE ALLOW ADVERSITY IN OUR LIVES?

Let's take a moment or two to consider some reasons.

1. Adversity levels us and keeps us humble.

Prosperity has a tendency to make people proud and self-sufficient. Though you might not say it in so many words, you really don't think you *need* God when you have your six-figure salary, or when your investments are going through the roof, or when your career is riding high, or when your family is healthy. But when the economy goes south, the stock market crashes, a home burns to the ground or your health fails, *then* you turn to God and are reminded of what really matters.

Prior to entering God's lush, beautiful Promised Land, the nation of Israel had endured forty years of wandering in a desolate wasteland, where they literally had to depend on God for breakfast, lunch, and dinner. Every day for four decades, the Lord had brought delicious manna to them, just outside their tent doors. But then they found themselves poised to enter a land of great abundance, "a land flowing with milk and honey" (Deuteronomy 6:3). That's when the Lord gave them this warning:

> When the Lord your God brings you into the land he swore to your fathers, to Abraham, Isaac and Jacob, to give you — a land with large, flourishing cities you did not build, houses filled with all kinds of good things you did not provide, wells you did not dig, and vineyards and olive groves you did not plant — then when you eat and are satisfied, be careful that you do not forget the Lord, who brought you out of Egypt, out of the land of slavery. (Deuteronomy 6:10-12, NIV)

That's what can happen sometimes. When you're prospering and healthy, and everything in life just seems to be sailing along, you can have a tendency to forget the Lord and take His kindness for granted.

Don't misunderstand what I'm saying here. I don't want to paint some bleak picture of life. If you find yourself in a season of green pastures and still waters, if your cup is running over, that's wonderful! Praise God for such times and seasons. Just be careful not to forget the Lord. Seek Him every day, hold all your possessions loosely, and always be sure to give Him glory.

But if the bottom drops out of your life and you get devastating news, I would say the same thing to you: Remember the Lord. Give Him glory. Turn to Him, call upon Him, and ask Him for help. There is no help like the help of the Lord.

2. Adversity teaches us eternal truths we would not otherwise learn.

Most of us want to avoid pain in life and be comfortable. We would love it if there were really such a thing as a painless dentist doing painless root canals. We would love a workout that didn't require us to sweat or get sore muscles. We would love a diet that allowed us to eat glazed doughnuts. We want the pounds to just melt off us, with no sacrifice or pain or hunger.

But it's just like that high school coach always told us: No pain, no gain. Pain comes into our lives and reminds us of our deeper needs. We need the Lord! In his book *The Problem of Pain*, C. S. Lewis writes, "[Pain] removes the veil; it plants the flag of truth within the fortress of a rebel soul."[2]

So God uses pain. Randy Alcorn writes, "If you base your faith on a lack of affliction, your faith lives on the brink of extinction and will fall apart because of a frightening diagnosis or a shattering phone call. Token faith will not survive suffering, nor should it."[3]

Listen, the faith that cannot be tested is a faith that cannot be trusted. God wants you to toughen up and grow up to be a man or woman of God. You can't be a baby in diapers for the rest of your life. Adversity grows us up in our faith and in the Lord.

3. Adversity gives us a new compassion for others who are in pain.

Let's face it, we live in a world of pain and hurt, and God comforts us so that we in turn can comfort others. Second Corinthians 1 says of the Lord,

> God is our merciful Father and the source of all comfort. He comforts us in all our troubles so that we can comfort others. When they are troubled, we will be able to give them the same comfort God has given us. For the more we suffer for Christ, the more God will shower us with his comfort through Christ. (verses 3-5, NLT)

When God brings you through a deep trial of some kind, you find yourself wanting to help someone else facing a similar trial. Let's say that you had cancer, went through a course of treatment, and have now been cancer-free for five years. Then you meet someone who has just received a diagnosis of cancer, and you can say, "Listen, I've been through this and come out on the other side. Let me encourage you. Let me pray for you." So you begin to comfort them with the same comfort the Lord has given you.

I find myself walking into a lot of situations these days that I previously would have walked away from. I've spoken with people who have lost a child or some other loved one. It's not like I have some deep, profound message for them. I just want to say to them, "As hard as it is to believe in this moment, you are going to get through this, and God will be with you." I just want to point them back to the Lord and to hope in Him.

Personal suffering is often a wakeup call to help us see the world's suffering. We have a greater sensitivity to it. After his wife died of cancer, C. S. Lewis said, "If I had really cared, as I thought I did, about the sorrows of the world, I should not have been so overwhelmed when my own sorrow came."[4]

4. Adversity prepares us for what God has ahead.

Everything we go through is preparation for something else in life. Through all these things, God is changing you and getting you ready for something ahead.

But here is what you need to remember. Your troubles, deep and painful as they may be to you now, won't last forever. In 2 Corinthians 4:17-18, Paul (who certainly had his share of troubles and heartaches) wrote,

> Our present troubles are small and won't last very long. Yet they produce for us a glory that vastly outweighs them and will last forever! So we don't look at the troubles we can see now; rather, we fix our gaze on things that cannot be seen. For the things we see now will soon be gone, but the things we cannot see will last forever. (NLT)

God's people will be better off eternally because they suffer temporarily. The tradeoff in eternity will bear this out.

The argument for the greater good may be the strongest biblical case for the whys of human suffering, but it requires great trust on our part. I have to look at my own suffering and say, "This doesn't make sense to me right now, but it's all going to make sense in eternity. It will produce something in eternity that would not have been there otherwise. So in faith I'm going to accept this truth and wait to see the outcome."

5. God can bring good out of the worst adversity.

In even the worst tragedy, we have a God who can bring good out of bad. That doesn't mean that He makes bad things good; it means that despite bad things, He can bring good. That's an important distinction, because a lot of times people are looking for cause and effect. They're trying to connect the dots, saying, "Well, a very bad thing happened to me so that this good thing could happen to me."

Sometimes life works that way, doesn't it? It certainly did for Joseph. Despite being betrayed by his brothers and falsely accused by his master's wife, he was elevated to the second most powerful position in all the world. And toward the end of the story, he even was able to say to his brothers, "As for you, you meant evil against me; but God meant it for good, in order to bring it about as it is this day, to save many people alive" (Genesis 50:20). So certainly God can do that.

In Romans 8:28, however, it says this: "We know that all things work together for good to those who love God, to those who are the called according to His purpose." Ultimately, all things work together for good, but sometimes you and I won't be able to see this in the course of our lifetimes. There are certain tragedies that will touch our lives that make no sense at all and won't until we get to heaven and learn the full story.

I think we make a big mistake when we try to find a cause and effect for every situation in life. Someone will say, "This teenager was tragically killed, but at the funeral three people came to Christ, so I guess it was worth it."

Guess what? God could have reached those three people without an individual being killed.

So let's look at it a different way. We say, "Someone has died, and I'm so sorry that happened. It's a real tragedy. But in spite of this terrible thing, look how God was glorified in the funeral service today and how three people came to Christ. Isn't that wonderful?"

Do you see the difference? If you're always trying to connect the dots and find cause and effect for every tragedy, you won't be able to do it. Some things simply will never make sense, and you might not see any "good" emerge from those circumstances for the rest of your life.

Just say, "This is what has happened, and it doesn't make sense to me. But I know that God is in control, that He loves me, and that He can even bring good out of this bad thing, for my life and His glory." It's very true. But we need to remember that some of that good will be realized in this life and some of it won't be realized until we're in heaven, in His presence.

Talk about worst-case scenarios. What could have been worse than the crucifixion of Jesus? It was the worst of the worst of the worst. One of His own disciples betrayed Him. He was questioned and manhandled by the Jewish leaders. Jesus was turned over to the Romans, who brutally scourged Him. Then He was crucified and left to die an agonizing death.

Horrible! Nothing could have been worse for His followers who had left everything to follow Him. But then He rose again from the dead, and it began to dawn on them what this new era and new covenant really meant.

And out of the very worst came the very best.

Out of the deepest darkness came the brightest of lights.

We now call that crucifixion day Good Friday, and that is what it was and is. To you and me, it means salvation from an eternal hell; salvation from an empty, purposeless life on earth; and an opportunity to live forever with Him and with all our loved ones who have trusted Him.

In the same way, on a much smaller scale, the crisis or tragedy you might be enduring right now ultimately will work together for good, either here or in eternity.

Sometimes you hear people say, "Hey, it's all good, man. It's all good." In many cases, that's just an empty expression; it means no more than "I'll be okay." But in a broader sense—in a theological sense—for the Christian, it *is* all good. Good will come from the hand of our good God and Savior, either in this life or in the life to come—and maybe both!

Shakespeare said that all the world's a stage and all the men and women are merely players. If that is true, then

God writes the script and has decided what will happen to whom and when it will happen.

The movies you and I remember are the ones that have conflict and where the hero overcomes in that conflict. What kind of story would it be if it started happy, stayed happy, and ended happy? We would be bored, wouldn't we? We would say, "Where's the conflict? Where's the bad guy? Where is the adversity that someone needs to overcome?" *Rocky* movies were perfect in that he always had so much to overcome—all that training and punching sides of beef in a meat locker and running up the steps. Then he takes on a villain in the ring and seems hopelessly outmatched. But that's what makes an exciting story. We like to see people with whom we identify overcoming long odds and great adversity.

That's a movie. But what about life?

When conflict comes, we realize that God is in charge of that conflict, from beginning to end. And He doesn't use conflict to make the story better but rather to make *us* better. If He allowed you to live a conflict-free life, you would no doubt end up as a soft, spoiled, selfish person. But if you have gone through adversity, that process tends to make you stronger, more capable, and hopefully more caring and sensitive to the troubles of others.

Sometimes God may stop the storm on our behalf, but no matter what, He always will be with us in the storm. As the prophet said, "His way is in the whirlwind and the storm, and clouds are the dust of his feet" (Nahum 1:3, NIV). He knows the way through the storm—any storm.

In the opening story of this chapter, Jesus stood up in the boat and commanded the wind and waves to be still, bringing about a wonderful calm. It's good to know that He *will* do that sometimes. Maybe you'll be going through some scary financial problem and cry out to God for help. Then in the next day or two, money arrives from some totally unexpected and unanticipated source, and it completely covers the amount of your need. In one way or another, God answers your prayer, and you say, "Lord, thank You!"

At other times, He may answer the prayer differently than you wanted Him to or expected Him to. He doesn't stop the storm or take away the problem or heal the illness, but He walks with you through it. Those are times when we must trust Him.

Again, if He has said to you, "Let's go to the other side of the lake," He will get you to the other side of the lake! It may not be through placid waters, but you will arrive:

> God is our refuge and strength,
> A very present help in trouble.
> Therefore we will not fear,
> Even though the earth be removed,
> And though the mountains be carried into the midst of the sea;
> Though its waters roar and be troubled,
> Though the mountains shake with its swelling. (Psalm 46:1-3)

Really, David? You won't even be afraid if the earth is removed? You won't be traumatized if great mountains start crashing into the sea? David had learned to trust his God no matter what.

In Isaiah 43, the Lord said,

> When you go through deep waters,
> I will be with you.
> When you go through rivers of difficulty,
> you will not drown.
> When you walk through the fire of oppression,
> you will not be burned up;
> the flames will not consume you.
> For I am the LORD, your God,
> the Holy One of Israel, your Savior. (verses 2-3, NLT)

Jesus had said, "Let's go over to the other side."

And that is just what you and I will do one day, and I don't mean the other side of the lake or even the other side of our problem. I mean that you and I will reach the Other Side: heaven itself. And then all the waves and wind and heartache and pain will be over. As Paul wrote in 1 Thessalonians 4:17, "We will be with the Lord forever" (NIV), which is even better than saying, "They lived happily ever after."

Storms will come and go, problems will come and go, and life on earth will come and go, but if you have put your faith in Christ, the end of life here will be the very beginning of the life that never ends.

CHAPTER TWO

HOPE FOR THOSE WHO HAVE LOST LOVED ONES

BECAUSE I NEVER HAD a father growing up and missed out on having a dad, I determined that if God ever gave me children, I would be Super Dad.

God did give Cathe and me children. Our son Christopher came along first, followed ten years later by his brother, Jonathan.

Did I really become Super Dad? No, I don't think I did. But I tried, and right from the start, I wanted to be a loving, present, hands-on father. I wanted to teach my boys the way of the Lord, but I wanted to have fun with them too.

Dr. James Dobson once said that every parent owes their first child an apology, and there is probably some truth in that statement. There is no question that I spoiled Christopher, buying him way too many cool toys. (But *I* got to play with them too.)

Christopher was a cute little boy who grew into a good-looking young man. As a child, he was precocious and always getting into trouble. In his twenties, he rebelled against the Lord, though he never was outwardly rebellious around his mother and me. All the same, we knew he was living a double life. We prayed for him constantly and spent many sleepless nights worrying about him and the direction of his life.

In time, God heard our prayers and got hold of Christopher's heart. He made a recommitment of his life to Christ, married Brittany, and began to serve the Lord. Not long afterward, our first granddaughter, Stella, was born. It was so exciting to be a grandparent. And then Christopher and Brittany were expecting their second child, little Lucy.

Our family's life changed, however, on a sunny summer day, July 24, 2008.

THE DAY OUR WORLD CHANGED

We were at home that morning. Cathe was doing a Bible study with Brittany and her mom, and I was watching Stella.

We had expected to hear from Christopher, who worked at Harvest Christian Fellowship and had left some time before. We tried to call him, but he didn't answer. I texted him, saying, "Where are you?" There was no answer.

There was a reason he didn't answer. My son left this world at 9:01 that morning and went immediately into the presence of God following an automobile crash.

I have no way of describing what that moment felt like. If you have ever lost a loved one suddenly and unexpectedly, you perhaps will understand. The word *devastated*—or even *crushed*—cannot come close to expressing it.

As a pastor with thirty years' experience, I have actually been with parents when they received news like that. I remember being with one anxious couple in a hospital waiting room while their daughter was undergoing an operation. When the surgeon came out, however, it was with the news that she hadn't survived the surgery. She had died on the operating table.

So I have been there with people in those circumstances and have seen their shock and grief up close as I tried to help them and minister to them.

I thought I knew what it was like.

But I really didn't.

You never know what it's like until it happens to you.

It's as though time just stops. It's as though the world stops spinning. I went into an immediate state of shock, literally collapsing on the floor. I don't even know if I cried. Reality stared me in the face, but I just couldn't believe it. *This isn't possible*, I told myself.

Almost immediately—seemingly within mere minutes—our home was filled with well-wishers, family, and friends. The phone rang off the hook and people rushed to us, seeking to bring help and comfort.

But it was all just a blur of noise to me. I didn't see anyone, didn't hear anyone's words. I managed to make my way to my office over our garage, fell on the floor, and cried aloud to God for help to get me through not the day but just the next few minutes.

I actually thought that if a person could die from hearing words, I could have died from what I had just heard. I remember thinking, *How can I survive this?* In the hours and days to come, I didn't want food and couldn't sleep. It was like living in a waking nightmare, where you're hoping with everything in you that you'll wake up and find it was all a bad dream.

So Friday passed, and Saturday came and went. On Sunday we said, "Let's go to church." People who saw us there couldn't believe it and said to me, "Oh, Greg, it was so *courageous* of you to come to church. You're such a model of faith."

The truth was, I came to church because I desperately needed God. It wasn't an example of great faith; it was an example of someone who felt weak in the extreme and needed help. So we sat in church that Sunday and listened to the teaching of the Word of God and worshipped the Lord.

At this writing, it has been three and a half years since that tragic day. Do I still mourn my son? Yes, I do. And it still hurts. In some ways, the passing of time has made things better, but the wound from that day in July was very deep and remains immensely painful. There is still a gaping hole in our lives that was once occupied by Christopher.

In the intervening time, however, I have learned much about grieving and loss. I have learned how to live with pain, how to cope with it. I'm now a member of a club I never wanted to join: someone who has suddenly and unexpectedly lost a close family member.

But I have also learned about something else in the last three and a half years. I have learned about hope. And I *have* hope. In fact, my hope today is stronger than it has been at any other time in my life. And that is why I felt compelled to write this book.

We all need hope, don't we? Hope is like an anchor that

keeps us in place through the tumultuous storms of life. In fact, Hebrews 6:19 says, "We have this hope as an anchor for the soul, firm and secure" (NIV).

The content of this book doesn't emerge from some ivory tower of theory. I haven't written it as a pastor who simply observed these hurts and wounds in the lives of others. No, these chapters come from the valley of the shadow of death, where I have personally found the hope promised to us in God's Word.

THE SOURCE OF HOPE

In Psalm 119:114, the psalmist wrote, "You are my refuge and my shield; your word is my source of hope" (NLT).

In the New Testament, the apostle Paul said, "Such things were written in the Scriptures long ago to teach us. And the Scriptures give us hope and encouragement as we wait patiently for God's promises to be fulfilled" (Romans 15:4, NLT).

It has been said that man can live forty days without food, three days without water, eight minutes without air, and about one second without hope. We all need hope in life to get through.

The presence of strong hope in your life, however, doesn't mean that you will somehow avoid pain on your journey. To have hope doesn't mean you have a permanent smile plastered on your face. Nor does it mean you experience some kind of spiritual lobotomy in which you no longer feel what other people feel. The fact is, hope and pain can coexist in your life, perhaps for a long time.

What, then, does it mean to have hope? Is it just hope in hope? Does it simply mean repeating to yourself over and over again, "Oh, I just know things will get better"? The truth is, circumstances may not get better; in fact, they could get worse.

So if we can't rely on circumstances, where do we place our hope?

"A FUTURE AND A HOPE"

We must place our hope in God, resting fully in Him. We must look to Him. One of my favorite verses about hope is in the Old Testament book of Jeremiah, where the Lord makes this statement:

> I know the thoughts that I think toward you, says the Lord, thoughts of peace and not of evil, to give you a future and a hope. (Jeremiah 29:11)

"To give you a future and a hope"—that is God's desire. That is what God is saying.

In context, God spoke those words to the Israelites when they were in Babylonian captivity. Because of their stubborn hearts and penchant for idolatry, the Lord had banished His people from Israel, their homeland, to the very heartland of pagan idolatry: Babylon. And they were there for seventy long years, just as the prophets had foretold.

In Babylon, they no longer had a temple where they could worship the God of Abraham, Isaac, and Jacob. One of the psalms, written in that period of captivity, says, "By the rivers of Babylon we sat and wept when we remembered

Zion. There on the poplars we hung our harps" (Psalm 137:1-2, NIV). Hanging their harps on the trees would be like putting away their guitars and unplugging their amps because there were no more praise services. And after a few years, they began to feel that God had abandoned them and forgotten all about them.

So with that backdrop, speaking to a displaced and discouraged people, the Lord said to them, "I know the thoughts that I think toward you . . . thoughts of peace and not of evil, to give you a future and a hope" (Jeremiah 29:11). In other words, God was saying to them, "Israel, listen to Me. Your days are not over. All has not been lost. I have a future for you." And God is saying the same to us.

I love how the Lord says, "I know the *thoughts* that I think toward you." It would have been enough if He had said, "I had a thought about you today. For one fleeting moment, you came to My mind." Even that would be amazing. To think that God Almighty, who exists both inside and outside of time and space, the Creator of the universe and all that is—to think that such a wondrous, majestic One as He would have a single thought about *me* during His day would be incredibly encouraging.

But that isn't what the Lord says here. He says something even more surprising than that. He declares, "I know the *thoughts*"—plural, more than one—"that I think toward you." And here's something more: He's not speaking in the past tense. He is thinking those thoughts *right now*, toward you! They are good thoughts, thoughts of peace and thoughts about your future and your hope.

The Bible says in Psalm 40:5,

> Many, O Lord my God, are Your wonderful works
> Which You have done;
> And Your thoughts toward us
> Cannot be recounted to You in order;
> If I would declare and speak of them,
> They are more than can be numbered.

In Psalm 139, David wrote, "How precious it is, Lord, to realize that you are thinking about me constantly! I can't even count how many times a day your thoughts turn toward me. And when I waken in the morning, you are still thinking of me!" (verses 17-18, TLB). Yes, He thinks thoughts about you—countless thoughts!

What does God mean when He says "a future"? It could better be translated "an expected end." Or another translation would be "a ground of hope" or "things hoped for." In other words, there will be an outcome. There will be completion in our lives. God will tie up the loose ends. And He needs to, because as imperfect followers of Jesus in an imperfect world, we are definitely works in progress.

A WORK IN PROGRESS

In addition to being a pastor, I'm also an artist. I didn't say I was a *good* artist, but I have always loved to draw. People who know that sometimes will ask me to draw something for them. I especially like to draw for little kids because they're always so appreciative and delighted by it.

I will sit down with someone and maybe draw a line or two and start to smile. The person will say, "Why are you smiling? There's nothing on the paper yet."

And I will say, "I'm just laughing about what I'm going to do. It's going to be a caricature of you, and you're going to look so funny!"

I haven't drawn hardly anything yet, but the picture is already complete in my mind. I already see it in my mind's eye.

We could think of God in the same way. Let's imagine Him working on a drawing. He draws one line, and we say, "Lord, what's that going to be? Finish it!"

But in God's mind, the art is done. The picture is complete. He has already seen it.

Though you are a work in progress, God knows exactly what He is doing. Romans 8:29 tells us that He is conforming us to the image of His own Son—line by line with a pencil, chip by chip with a chisel. There is an expected end to our lives, and it is good.

You might read the above paragraph and reply to me, "Wait a minute, Greg. What about when nothing in life seems to make sense? What about when we get sick and pray to be healed, and we're not healed? What about when someone dies? Where is that 'good' you're talking about? Where is that expected end now?"

It's called heaven.

Nobody said that life here on earth would be all sunny, warm, and strewn with rose petals. Yes, in God's grace and kindness, you will have good moments in this life, perhaps many of them. There will be seasons when everything seems to come together and make sense. But there also will be those times when things don't make sense at all. Ultimately, however, the future for every believer is being in the presence of God in heaven.

That is our ultimate hope. And God is the One in whom we place our total trust and confidence.

Psalm 38:15 says, "In You, O Lord, I hope; You will hear, O Lord my God."

And in Psalm 130:5, we read, "I am counting on the Lord; yes, I am counting on him. I have put my hope in his word" (NLT).

Now, this all sounds quite sunny and happy. But here is what I want you to understand: You can be in mourning and hopeful at the same time.

IN MOURNING . . . AND IN HOPE

When a loved one leaves this world—especially when the departure is sudden and unexpected—it tears us up inside. Even when we expect the death to come and have tried to prepare ourselves in some measure, it is still very difficult to deal with. There is a deep sense of loss because there was a deep love.

Sometimes people will say, "You shouldn't be crying. You shouldn't be mourning. If that person was a believer, then he's in heaven. He's with the Lord." But even the great apostle Paul talked about feeling deep sorrow over the prospect of a close friend dying:

> I thought I should send Epaphroditus back to you. He is a true brother, co-worker, and fellow soldier. And he was your messenger to help me in my need. I am sending him because he has been longing to see you, and he was very distressed that you heard he was ill. And he certainly was ill; in

> fact, he almost died. But God had mercy on him — and also on me, so that I would not have one sorrow after another. (Philippians 2:25-27, NLT)

Paul speaks of unbearable sorrow over a fellow believer dying? Really? Isn't this the same Paul who already had been to heaven and came back again? Isn't this the same Paul who had more faith than anyone you could imagine? Yet Paul himself was saying that if Epaphroditus had died, he didn't know how he could have endured it.

That's how it can be sometimes. You think to yourself, *Can I get through this? Can I actually survive?* People will say to you (and you can count on this), "Stop crying. Get a grip! Get over it."

Don't *ever* say that to someone in mourning!

Don't ever set yourself up as a judge of when someone else's season of grieving and mourning ought to be over. Who are you to say such a thing? Who are you to make such a judgment? You are out of bounds when you do so. The Bible says there is a time to weep and a time to mourn, and it will work itself out in different ways for different people.

I cringe when I think back on some of the things I've said over the years to people who were grieving. I said things in my impatience to see them get better. I had imagined that I had their best interests in mind. But I didn't really know what I was talking about. You need to give a grieving person time.

Mourning is part of the healing process. I know people who have lost loved ones who never dealt with their grief properly or mourned as they should have. Sometimes they were in a state of denial, where they simply wouldn't acknowledge what happened, or they wouldn't let go of the person who had gone on and it changed who they were.

You need to grieve. You need to let it out. And though you may want to fight them, tears have their place. When I speak about weeping, I mean really crying hard. It's not when you get a lump in your throat or your eyes mist up a little; it's when you cry so hard that you feel pain in your chest and maybe even drop to the ground.

Believe it or not, *that* kind of mourning can be healing.

So be patient with people who are experiencing grief.

YOU NEED PERSPECTIVE

What do you need as someone who is mourning the loss of a loved one? You need perspective.

The psalmist wrote,

> Day and night I have only tears for food,
>   while my enemies continually taunt me, saying,
>   "Where is this God of yours?"
>
> My heart is breaking
>   as I remember how it used to be:
> I walked among the crowds of worshipers,
>   leading a great procession to the house of God,
> singing for joy and giving thanks —
>   it was the sound of a great celebration! (42:3-4, NLT)

But then the psalmist corrected himself and said,

> Why am I discouraged?
>   Why is my heart so sad?

> I will put my hope in God!
> I will praise him again —
> my Savior and my God! (verses 5-6, NLT)

I know what the psalmist meant when he said, "I have only tears for food." I know what it means to lose your appetite and have a breakfast, lunch, and dinner of tears. My wife told me she had seen me cry maybe two or three times in our life together. But after the Lord took Christopher, I cried hard every day for hours at a time.

Then there were those times when I seemingly would go into a black hole. It happens like this: You're just going about your life doing the necessary things, and something triggers a memory. It's ridiculous how many things can do that! And suddenly you remember a time when you and your loved one were together. Your first instinct in that moment is to call him or her, but then you realize you can't. It hits you all over again, and you say, "They're gone. Gone! I never will see them on this earth again! Why did this happen to me?"

Did you imagine that preachers don't go through such things? You're wrong. I'm just a man, a human being, and those were the kind of thoughts that would surge through my mind.

So that's when I do what the writer of Psalm 42 did: I start talking to myself. I will say, "Hold it, Greg. Now you listen to me!" (Someone watching would think I am a lunatic, and maybe I am. But I'm a *hopeful* lunatic.) I will say, "Greg, listen up! The Bible says that your son is in heaven and that you *will* see him again. (Are you listening, Greg?) And the Bible says that Jesus is the resurrection and the life and that he who believes in Him will not die! Do you remember those verses, Greg? Well, think of them again!"

In those moments, I will quote verses out loud and remind myself of the promises of God. And guess what? It works. It lifts me up from this pit into which I've stumbled.

WIPEOUT

Where I live, in Southern California, some people identify with surfing illustrations. And grief is a lot like wiping out on a big wave. I get out to the beach with a board now and then, and I would like to say that I'm a great surfer. That's what I would *like* to say. Actually, I do a lot more floundering in white water than I do surfing.

What you want to avoid is getting caught in the impact zone of a wave. So when you're out surfing and see a set of waves coming in, you have to do the very thing you don't want to do, which is to head directly toward the wave. What you *want* to do — if the wave is really big and you're afraid of it — is paddle like crazy for shore. But that would be a mistake, because the wave would catch you and throw you around. What you need to do is swim toward the wave and try to go under it or over the top of it.

If a wave crashes over the top of you, you can get seriously discombobulated, so much so that you literally don't know which way is up. Many swimmers and surfers have drowned because they were mixed up and went the wrong direction. They went down when they should have gone up. Then they take water into their lungs, go unconscious, and find themselves standing before God.

So here is what you need to remember if you're out with your surfboard or boogie board and have a leash going from your board and attached to your ankle. If you find yourself smashed by a wave and pushed underwater, grab your leash, pull on it, and go in the direction of the leash. Why? Because it's attached to your board, your board is buoyant, and it will head toward the surface. So even if it goes against the logic of the moment, follow your leash to the top.

Here is the analogy, then: The Word of God is like that leash we pull on. And if we stay attached to it and follow it, it will take us to the surface, where we can get proper perspective on what is really happening. Our emotions, turbulent as white water, will get the best of us and overwhelm us at times. But because we hope in God and believe in the Word of God, we get our perspective back and find help and correction. Yes, another big wave will come—and another and another after that. But like following that leash to a surfboard that pops up out of the swirling water, we keep coming back to hope, again and again and again.

TWO SISTERS REGAIN PERSPECTIVE

In John 11, we have the story of a little family who had lost a loved one—and almost lost hope. It tells the story of the passing of a man named Lazarus and how his two sisters, Mary and Martha, regained their perspective. It is also a story of how Jesus reacts—and how God can be glorified in such situations.

Mary, Martha, and Lazarus were a tight-knit little family: three siblings who loved each other and had made a great home together. Everyone knew that Martha was a killer chef, and Jesus loved to come visit, showing up with twelve friends! Martha, who always was so welcoming and hospitable, would throw together a fantastic meal for the Lord and His men. All three members of this family could legitimately say that Jesus of Nazareth was their personal friend because He frequented their home in Bethany, which was conveniently located near Jerusalem.

Tragedy came to their home, however, just as it comes to all of our homes. Lazarus became very ill. In fact, it looked as though he might not make it.

That's where the story starts:

> Now a certain man was sick, Lazarus of Bethany, the town of Mary and her sister Martha. It was that Mary who anointed the Lord with fragrant oil and wiped His feet with her hair, whose brother Lazarus was sick. Therefore the sisters sent to Him, saying, "Lord, behold, he whom You love is sick." (John 11:1-3)

WHAT DO WE LEARN FROM THIS STORY?

1. Life is filled with pain, sorrow, and the death of loved ones.

I don't know why, but some of us may imagine that we're going to get a pass. We have actually convinced ourselves that we will somehow make it through life unscathed, never having to face a major tragedy, never suffering from a serious illness, and never losing a loved one.

But then when one of these events arrives on our doorstep, we're stunned! We're shocked and amazed that such a thing could happen to us.

We shouldn't be.

In 1 Peter 4:12, the apostle wrote, "Dear friends, do not be surprised at the painful trial you are suffering, as though something strange were happening to you" (NIV).

Why would you be surprised because you find yourself in a "painful trial"? Painful trials happen to everyone. Jesus said, "In the world you will have tribulation; but be of good cheer, I have overcome the world" (John 16:33).

Tribulations, painful trials, and even tragedies will come your way in this life. Death eventually will knock at your door too. It probably will start with your grandparents dying and then your parents. You might have a close friend die. Eventually, it could be a sibling, a spouse, or even a child. When it's someone close to you, in your very family circle, it will have a profound impact on you, as it did Mary and Martha.

2. God loves us.

Don't misunderstand that statement, and don't rush over it. Let it sink in. God loves you! And because He does, whatever He does or allows to happen in your life as His child has been filtered through and is motivated by that love. God says in His Word, "I have loved you with an everlasting love; therefore with lovingkindness I have drawn you" (Jeremiah 31:3). He loves you. And He loved Mary, Martha, and Lazarus.

I want you to notice what they said in John 11:3: "Lord, behold, he whom You love is sick."

They knew Jesus loved them. The term that was translated "he whom You love" is from the Greek word *phileo*, meaning "brotherly love." (That's where Philadelphia, the City of Brotherly Love, got its name.) So the message said,

"Lord, Your friend, whom You love like a brother, is sick."

They sent that message to Jesus, and they did the right thing! That is the perfect thing to do when any kind of crisis hits. Whenever you find yourself in trouble of any kind, bring it to Jesus. That ought to be our first inclination, our immediate reflex.

When the Israelites turned against Moses in Exodus 15:25, "he cried out to the LORD." It's the best thing you can ever do. When you are criticized unfairly, take it to the Lord.

When Hezekiah received a threatening letter, he took it into the temple and spread it out before the Lord. When John the Baptist was beheaded, the disciples went and told Jesus. So that's what we need to do when trouble disturbs our peace or darkens our horizon: We need to go and tell Jesus.

I want you to notice the basis for their appeal. They didn't say, "Hey, Lord, You owe us one! Think of all the times we housed You and fed You and took care of Your disciples. Think of the refuge we provided and the friendship we offered You. How about showing a little love here and healing Your friend?" They didn't say anything like that. They just said, "Lord, the one that You love is sick."

They didn't even say, "Lord, we love You so much, so do this for us." They did not base their appeal on their love for God but rather on His love for them. That is just what we should do. Our love is fickle and fluctuates, but God's love for us is consistent and never changes.

Look at John 11:4-5: "When Jesus heard that, He said, 'This sickness is not unto death, but for the glory of God, that the Son of God may be glorified through it.' Now Jesus loved Martha and her sister and Lazarus. So, when He heard that he was sick, He stayed two more days in the place where He was."

He did *what*? He stayed *where*? Why didn't He find the fastest horse in town and gallop full speed to their house to help His sick friend? Why did He delay His arrival at such a crucial moment? Since He loved them, why didn't He hurry?

John used two different words for *love* in this passage. Mary and Martha said, "The one you love [*phileo*, brother love] is sick." But when it speaks of Jesus' love for Martha, Mary, and Lazarus, the Bible uses the Greek word *agape*, which speaks of God's all-consuming love. And Jesus, *because* He loved him in this way, did not come when they wanted Him to come.

Remember this: His delays are not necessarily His denials. Just as surely as God has His will, He has His timing. Ecclesiastes 3:11 says, "He has made everything beautiful in its time."

So here is what was really happening: Jesus wanted to help Mary and Martha see a bigger picture. He was saying, in essence, "I know it seems to you like I should come there right now. I understand that. But what I intend to do will be better than what you are asking Me to do. I will answer you above and beyond your request."

By the time He finally showed up, however, things were looking pretty bleak. Lazarus wasn't sick anymore—he was dead. Because he had been in his tomb for four days already, decomposition had set in. Jesus not only missed the opportunity to heal His friend but even missed his funeral!

When Martha saw Jesus coming down the road toward her, she couldn't help letting her hurt feelings and perplexity boil over a little:

> Now Martha, as soon as she heard that Jesus was coming, went and met Him, but Mary was sitting in the house. Now Martha said to Jesus, "Lord, if You had been here, my brother would not have died. But even now I know that whatever You ask of God, God will give You."
>
> Jesus said to her, "Your brother will rise again."
>
> Martha said to Him, "I know that he will rise again in the resurrection at the last day."
>
> Jesus said to her, "I am the resurrection and the life. He who believes in Me, though he may die, he shall live. And whoever lives and believes in Me shall never die. Do you believe this?" (John 11:20-26)

Martha may have had major questions in her heart, but she did the right thing. She didn't run *from* Jesus; she ran *to* Him with her broken heart. And that is what we need to do as well.

Sometimes you will hear people say, "Don't ever ask God why." Where do they get that stuff? The truth is, you can ask God why as much as you want. He might not answer you right away, but there's nothing wrong with asking the question. Ask away! Be honest with God, and tell Him your heart. That's what David did. He wrote in Psalm 62, "Trust in him at all times, O people; pour out your hearts to him, for God is our refuge" (verse 8, NIV).

Because God already sees your heart, tell Him exactly what you are feeling. Say, "God, I'm not happy right now. I don't understand this at all. I'm hurting, and none of this makes any sense to me. Why did You allow this to happen?"

Is that blasphemy?

Of course not.

Jesus Himself said from the cross, "My God, My God, why have You forsaken Me?" Was *that* blasphemy? No! He was calling on His Father. And again and again in the psalms, we can see the psalmists telling God exactly how they're feeling and how the world looks to them in that moment.

That is the *right* thing to do. They're calling on God. They're seeking God. They're reaching out to God. That is what we need to do in our times of sorrow and pain and perplexity. Don't withdraw from God; connect with Him. Cry out to Him.

In the book of Job, after Job had heard the horrible news of the death of his children, he worshipped God and said, "Naked I came from my mother's womb, and naked I will depart. The LORD gave and the LORD has taken away; may the name of the LORD be praised" (Job 1:21, NIV).

Yet as you read through Job's story, you can see that he asked God why many times. And he never really got an explanation:

> Why did I not perish at birth, and die as I came from the womb? (3:11, NIV)
>
> Why is light given to a man whose way is hidden, and whom God has hedged in? (3:23, NIV)
>
> Will You not look away from me, and let me alone? (7:19, NIV)
>
> Why do You hide Your face, and regard me as Your enemy? (13:24)

The questions went on and on.

But even if God were to answer all our whys and try to explain things to us, it would quickly blow our minds. It would be like trying to wire a lightning bolt to a flashlight bulb. We wouldn't be able to handle it!

The truth is, we live on promises, not explanations. It

really doesn't help us to keep asking why, why, why. Instead, we should be asking *what,* as in, *What do I do now, Lord? What is Your will for me now?* We need to turn to Him and wait on Him.

After Martha met with Jesus, her sister Mary went to see Him:

> When Mary came where Jesus was, and saw Him, she fell down at His feet, saying to Him, "Lord, if You had been here, my brother would not have died."
>
> Therefore, when Jesus saw her weeping, and the Jews who came with her weeping, He groaned in the spirit and was troubled. And He said, "Where have you laid him?"
>
> They said to Him, "Lord, come and see." (John 11:32-34)

This is followed by verse 35, the shortest verse in the Bible: "Jesus wept." That brings us to a third point.

3. Jesus weeps with us in our time of pain.

Yes, Jesus was and is the Son of God, coequal with the Father and the Holy Spirit, filled with power and glory. But He also walked this earth as a real man who felt our pain and sorrows. Isaiah 53 says,

> We despised him and rejected him — a man of sorrows, acquainted with bitterest grief. We turned our backs on him and looked the other way when he went by. He was despised, and we didn't care. Yet it was our grief he bore, our sorrows that weighed him down. (verses 3-4, TLB)

Yes, He understands our grief. He voluntarily put Himself in the way of danger, torture, and death to bear our sorrows on the cross. Why would He do this? Hebrews 2:17-18 gives the answer:

> It was necessary for him to be made in every respect like us, his brothers and sisters, so that he could be our merciful and faithful High Priest before God. Then he could offer a sacrifice that would take away the sins of the people. Since he himself has gone through suffering and testing, he is able to help us when we are being tested. (NLT)

If something breaks your heart, it breaks His as well.

Scripture reminds us that God keeps our tears in a bottle: "You keep track of all my sorrows. You have collected all my tears in your bottle. You have recorded each one in your book" (Psalm 56:8, NLT).

When I was in Israel in 2008 before our son died, we visited a Jewish antiquities store I had heard about, with relics dating back three thousand years. It was like a museum, except they would let you hold things. As I looked around, I saw fragments of pottery and other items that were hundreds and even thousands of years old. But then, standing out in the midst of all of those antiquities, I saw a beautiful, translucent blue bottle.

"Sir," I asked the owner of the store, "what is this blue bottle?"

"Oh," he said, "that is a Roman tear bottle."

"Really? I've never heard of that. What's it for?"

"The Romans believed that when they lost a loved one, if they put their tears in a bottle, they would be recorded in heaven."

I was immediately reminded of these words from the psalmist: "You have collected all my tears in your bottle."

I have a tear bottle also. (I didn't buy the one in Jerusalem. It was too expensive!) My tear bottle is in heaven, where God keeps record of every tear I have ever shed. He keeps track of your tears too. And He promises that when we are finally in His presence, He will wipe every tear from our eyes (see Revelation 21:4).

The story about Jesus and His friends continues: "Jesus was still angry as he arrived at the tomb, a cave with a stone rolled across its entrance" (John 11:38, NLT).

Why was Jesus angry? Was He angry with all the mourners who were weeping and wailing? Absolutely not. He felt compassion for them and even wept with them.

No, Jesus was angry with death itself. This was not the way it was meant to be. Death should never have come into our world, nor should have aging, disability, or disease. Death is an aberration from God's intended order. But because of man's sin, the curse of death fell on God's creation. And Jesus was angry about that. But even in the face of death and tragedy, He was about to show forth the glory of God.

4. God can be glorified through human suffering, bringing good out of bad.

Most of us are familiar with the story. Jesus had the stone rolled away from the front of the tomb and with a commanding voice called His friend out of the tomb and back from the dead.

Honestly, you have to feel a little sorry for Lazarus. Called back to Earth after spending four days in heaven? What a disappointment! That would be like trying to get a kid out of Disneyland who has been there for only ten minutes.

But Lazarus had no choice, because Jesus, the Lord of

life, called to him from the other side. It's a good thing Jesus said, "*Lazarus*, come out," because if He had simply said, "Come out," everyone in every grave in the world would have come out.

The bad thing for Lazarus was that he just had to die again, a few years down the road. As if it weren't bad enough to die once, he had to die twice! Nevertheless, God was glorified by that miracle on that day, just as Jesus said He would be.

Here's the part we need to remember: Sometimes God is glorified through the removal of affliction, and sometimes He is glorified when His people endure affliction, trusting in Him. When you have some medical problem and God delivers you, through the hands of a surgeon or through a miraculous healing, it's a wonderful thing, a cause for celebration and joy, and our hearts overflow with gratitude and praise.

But it doesn't always happen that way, does it?

There are times when the surgery doesn't go as hoped, when the illness isn't removed, and when the problem isn't taken away. In those instances, God gains glory when His people patiently endure the suffering and sorrow, turning to Him and trusting in Him.

In fact, it is through hardship that we develop our faith and hope, like a muscle encountering resistance, being exercised, and gaining strength.

You would *think* the best way to find hope would be to have a trouble-free life, but that's not true. The best way to find hope is through the crises of life. Romans 5:3-5 says it like this:

> We can rejoice, too, when we run into problems and trials, for we know that they help us develop endurance. And endurance develops strength of character, and character strengthens our confident hope of salvation. And this hope will not lead to disappointment. For we know how dearly God loves us, because he has given us the Holy Spirit to fill our hearts with his love. (NLT)

Hope comes through hardship. So when a Christian suffers and still trusts God and gives Him glory, it reassures the rest of us that there never will be a valley so deep that God won't get us through it.

It also reminds us that death isn't the end. We may know this as a fact, but we need to be reminded again and again. Physical death is not the end of existence; it is just a change in the state of existence. The tomb isn't the entrance to death but rather the entrance to life. Heaven is the earthly life of the believer, glorified and perfected. When a believer dies, he or she goes immediately into God's presence.

And that is the *ultimate* hope.

Do you have that hope? What are you hoping in? Everyone hopes in something. Some maybe hope in themselves. Like Maria in *The Sound of Music*, some say, "I have confidence in confidence alone." Really? How long will that last? That won't sustain you when great trials and hardships roll across your life.

Others place their hope in technology or even politicians. But these won't help you when you're facing the death of a loved one. Put your hope in God! He will never let you down.

The Bible says that is true, and I personally *know* that it is true because I have put it to the test. God has been there for me, and He will be there for you. No matter what you may face in life, He will walk with you through it. Remember the twenty-third psalm: "Yea, though I walk through the valley of the shadow of death, I will fear no evil; for You are with me."

As you face the great hurts, disappointments, and sorrows of life, you will be either hopeful or hopeless. Proverbs 10:28 says, "The hopes of the godly result in happiness, but the expectations of the wicked come to nothing" (NLT).

Hope in God.

As Christians, no matter what happens in life, we have the guaranteed assurance that when we die, we will go to heaven.

That's the biggest win-win that ever was.

CHAPTER THREE

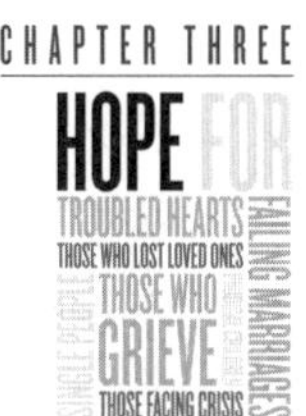

HOPE FOR LONELY HEARTS

WHAT ARE YOU LOOKING for most in life?

An extensive survey that asked this very question was recently concluded by a leading polling agency, with questionnaires distributed to people of various ages and occupations.

After compiling the results, the analysts were surprised. Most of them imagined answers suggesting more materialistic goals: a bigger house, a nicer car, a more prestigious job. But what was at the top of the list?

Love.

Most people want to love and be loved more than anything else in life.

What is love? For many people, love equals lust, and that's about all they understand. Where, then, do we turn for a fuller understanding of love?

If you're looking to our contemporary culture, you'll be disappointed. If you're looking to Hollywood for examples of how to have a lasting and meaningful relationship, that is not going to work at all. If you're listening to popular music, you won't get much help there, either.

I actually did an online search for all the songs with the word *love* in them, looked at the results for a while, and began arranging them a little. First of all, there is the classic song that says, "What the world needs now is love, sweet love." So this basically establishes that everyone is looking for it. Then the group Foreigner sang, "I want to know what love is." Go back a few years and you have that enduring classic, "Yummy, yummy, yummy, I've got love in my tummy."

One song tells us that love is "a many-spendored thing." Another says that "love is the answer." Led Zeppelin sang about a whole lot of love. Meatloaf declared that he would do anything for love. Phil Collins, however, warned us that you can't hurry love. And why is that? Another song tells us, "That's the way love goes."

So let's put this all together and review. What have we learned so far? We need love in our tummy . . . because love is the answer . . . it's many splendored . . . and we need a whole lot of it. But you can't hurry it, because . . . that's the way love goes.

Frankly. I don't find a lot of help in that summary.

What we truly need is authentic love, not the wispy, wishy-washy, pseudo love of today's culture.

LONELINESS AND LONGINGS

You may be experiencing loneliness in your life because you're single. Sometimes you wonder whether you will ever find that person to marry and spend the rest of your life with. But guess what? Single people aren't the only ones who are lonely. Did you know there are lonely married people too?

Finding yourself in a loveless marriage might be the loneliest place of all. Some people have a mate who has become so disengaged or self-absorbed that he or she isn't even trying anymore in the marriage. Still others may be believers who are married to unbelievers and can't share with their mate the deepest and most important thoughts, feelings, and desires in their life.

Loneliness, then, can happen with both unmarried and married people.

One of our biggest mistakes in the first place is assuming that marriage will somehow solve all of our problems.

I raised two sons, but I now have four granddaughters and have entered an amazing new world of pink and glitter and princesses and ponies and mermaids. I can now tell you with authority that little girls really do like the color pink (it's right up there with purple), and they love to dress up like little princesses.

I've noticed that even at a very early age, there is a longing in the heart of a little girl that someday her prince will come. Some people enter into their adult years and never quite get over these fantasies; they're still looking for a perfect princess or a noble prince. They're still waiting for a man or woman to come along who will make them happy or "complete them."

A Hollywood actress recently said, "I believe a lot of us feel there is a big hole in our hearts, an unfortunate ache that is fixed by some people eating too much, others with drugs. In my case, I am a romance junkie."

Let's just start with this simple truth: You need to be

content where you are, regardless of your marital status. If you are single, you need to be content as single, and if you are married, you need to be content as a married person. The fact is that no other human being on the planet—no matter how considerate, kind, and wonderful—will be able to fill all of those needs, hopes, and expectations in your heart. (And it is unrealistic and unfair to expect that of *any* person.) No man or woman has the capacity to satisfy the deep-down aches and longings God has placed within the human soul. Only a relationship with God Himself can accomplish that. He is the One we need, first and foremost, single or married. As Solomon wrote, "He has planted eternity in the human heart" (Ecclesiastes 3:11, NLT). That eternal longing within you can be met only by the Eternal One.

The woman Jesus met at the well in Sychar (see John 4) had to find that out. She may have been an attractive woman—no doubt she was, having attracted five different men as husbands (not to mention the guy she was currently living with, who wasn't her husband). On that hot midday in Samaria, Jesus used the town's well as a metaphor for life. He said, "Whoever drinks of this water will thirst again" (verse 13). In other words, He was saying, "Lady, let Me tell you something: Living with all these different men isn't going to meet the deepest need of your life. That's why you keep moving from one guy to another. But if you drink of the water that I will give, you won't be thirsty again."

In Philippians 4:11, the apostle Paul wrote, "I have learned to be content whatever the circumstances" (NIV). Hebrews 13:5 says, "Let your conduct be without covetousness; be content with such things as you have. For He Himself has said, 'I will never leave you nor forsake you.'"

So it is the Lord we need, first and foremost. We need to find our contentment and happiness in our relationships with Him. In Romans 12:12, Paul wrote, "Base your happiness on your hope in Christ" (PH). In Psalm 37:4, David declared, "Delight yourself also in the LORD, and He shall give you the desires of your heart."

Note that it doesn't say here, "Delight yourself also in the LORD, and He will give you a spouse." He will give you the desires of your heart; in other words, He will fill your heart with the right desires. So first find your fulfillment in Christ Himself, base your happiness in your daily walk with Him, and then wait on Him. Don't be obsessed with finding a mate; instead, focus your energy on seeking God. I believe that if you do, in His timing He will bring that right person to you. Jesus said, "Seek the Kingdom of God above all else, and live righteously, and he will give you everything you need" (Matthew 6:33, NLT).

Nevertheless, it is far better to be happily single than unhappily married. Comedian Chris Rock said, "You can be married and bored, or single and lonely." Are those the only choices, Chris? I don't think so! If marriage is miserable, then the fault lies with the participants, not the institution.

WHY LIVING TOGETHER IS WRONG

Some singles subscribe to the opinion that married people are generally unhappy. They reason as follows: 50 percent of all marriages end in divorce, and probably 50 percent of all who stay married are miserable. So why get married?

Some in today's culture are saying that the whole

institution of marriage is outdated. In a recent poll of singles, 40 percent said that they thought marriage was obsolete. Many will say, "Why don't we just live together instead? Everybody's doing it. Why bother with marriage? Isn't it just a piece of paper? What does it really mean?"

That may sound logical to some people, but it is not correct on the facts. Statistics say that living together will hurt, not help, your chance of eventually having a happy marriage. The Census Bureau informs us that there are one million unmarried couples now living together—a 600 percent increase in this last decade. Fewer people are getting married these days, and if that trend continues, a minority of adults will be married in the next few years.

But here is why living together is wrong: First and foremost, it is a sin against God.

Living together outside of marriage is a violation of God's order as revealed in Scripture, and He will not bless it. This means that every day you live this way, you are effectively separated from fellowship with God. So if you care at all about getting closer to God, finding forgiveness of sin, and benefiting from His wisdom, favor, guidance, protection, and blessing in your life, living together is not the answer.

But what about all of those unhappy marriages? Yes, we all know of married couples who aren't happy or can't seem to get along. But the real truth here is that married people truly are the happiest people. In his book *The Meaning of Marriage*, author Timothy Keller wrote,

> All surveys tell us that the number of people who say they are "*very* happy" in their marriage is high — about 61–62 percent — and there

> has been little decrease in this figure during the last decade. Most striking of all, longitudinal studies demonstrate that two-thirds of those unhappy marriages out there will become happy within five years if people stay married and do not get divorced. . . . During the last two decades the great preponderance of research evidence shows that people who are married consistently show much higher degrees of satisfaction with their lives than those who are single, divorced, or living with a partner.[1]

THOUGHTS ABOUT THE SINGLE LIFE

Yes, there are clear advantages to being married, but there are advantages to remaining single as well. Paul lays it out pretty clearly in 1 Corinthians 7:32-35:

> I want you to live as free of complications as possible. When you're unmarried, you're free to concentrate on simply pleasing the Master. Marriage involves you in all the nuts and bolts of domestic life and in wanting to please your spouse, leading to so many more demands on your attention. The time and energy that married people spend on caring for and nurturing each other, the unmarried can spend in becoming whole and holy instruments of God. I'm trying to be helpful and make it as easy as possible for you, not make things harder. (MSG)

Paul isn't critical of a married person's wanting to please his or her spouse—that's what you *should* seek to do. But when you are single, you don't have that responsibility. You have flexibility and mobility and can do things many married people can't. This is especially helpful when it comes to serving the Lord. If you keep your lifestyle simple and don't load yourself down with a lot of material possessions, you have a remarkable freedom to pick up and go somewhere—anywhere—to meet various needs in the body of Christ all over the world. As a single, you can seize and utilize opportunities to serve more easily than a married individual.

There are some people who feel as though they never want to get married and can remain single all their lives and happily so. That is absolutely fine. To our knowledge, the apostle Paul was never married. Neither was our Lord Jesus. There is a life God can give you as a single person that can be very fulfilling, not to mention free and unburdened.

If, on the other hand, you long for a mate, don't despair: Chances are you will get married someday. Studies show that nine out of ten Americans are married at least at some point in their lives.

So what do you do in the meantime? You can start praying for your future mate. You might not even know who that person is. Then again, you might know that individual but have never really considered him or her as a potential mate. You have a friendship with someone of the opposite sex, and perhaps one day you look at that person and something dawns on you: *Maybe this is who I've been looking for.*

What should you be looking for in a potential mate? I saw a survey not long ago among singles that asked for the single most important quality they were looking for in a mate. Number one was beauty or good looks. Number two was brains. Number three was disposable cash. It's interesting to me that no mention is made of inner qualities: kindness, faithfulness, patience, or a sense of humor. After being married thirty-eight years, I still appreciate my wife's beauty, but it's the inner qualities that really matter in the long run.

Typically, women worry a great deal more about beauty

and the inevitable marks of aging than men do. I see nothing wrong with a woman seeking to look as attractive as she can through the years, but the best goal is to seek to be a woman of virtue.

Proverbs 31 says, "Who can find a virtuous and capable wife? She is more precious than rubies. Her husband can trust her, and she will greatly enrich his life. She brings him good, not harm, all the days of her life" (verses 10-12, NLT). Later we read, "Charm is deceptive, and beauty does not last; but a woman who fears the LORD will be greatly praised" (verse 30, NLT).

Sometimes we think of the word *virtue* as a feminine word, but in the original language, it is not feminine at all. Sometimes the root word for virtue is used to describe an army! The word doesn't speak of femininity as much as it speaks of strength, power, and influence. So the Bible is actually saying, "Be a woman of strength, be a woman of influence, as God has given you a skill set to influence others in a profound and significant way."

The apostle Peter calls on women to cultivate inner qualities of beauty rather than be preoccupied with their appearance. Peter wrote,

> Don't be concerned about the outward beauty of fancy hairstyles, expensive jewelry, or beautiful clothes. You should clothe yourselves instead with the beauty that comes from within, the unfading beauty of a gentle and quiet spirit, which is so precious to God. (1 Peter 3:3-4, NLT)

Many young women in our contemporary culture don't even give a passing thought to the inner person. That is why, by contrast, Christian girls are so attractive, and that is also why some non-Christian girls will sometimes try to attack or slander the girls who love and follow the Lord. A woman who follows the Lord has a special quality that shines right through the outer, physical appearance. It's a magnetic beauty that women who don't know the Lord simply can't match or compete with.

Why not give at least equal time to your spiritual life as you give to your physical life? Spend as much time in Bible study and prayer as you spend in working out or being in front of a mirror. As Paul wrote to Timothy, "Physical training is good, but training for godliness is much better, promising benefits in this life and in the life to come" (1 Timothy 4:8, NLT).

Just be the best you that you can be. There is a place for cultivating your outward appearance—nice clothes, make-up, hairstyles, and staying in shape. There is nothing wrong with looking attractive within the bounds of modesty and good taste. Just don't neglect the spiritual part of your life, which is even more important. In fact, it will last forever.

WHAT QUALITIES ARE MOST IMPORTANT?

I am asked all the time, "Greg, is it okay to enter into a dating relationship or potentially romantic relationship with a nonbeliever?"

In a word, no.

In 2 Corinthians 6, Paul said,

> Don't team up with those who are unbelievers. How can righteousness be a partner with wickedness? How can light live with darkness? What harmony

> can there be between Christ and the devil? How can a believer be a partner with an unbeliever? And what union can there be between God's temple and idols? For we are the temple of the living God. (verses 14-16, NLT)

Someone will say, "I want to reach this person for the Lord. If I have a relationship with him, I'm going to win him to Christ."

That's what we call famous last words.

In fact, so-called missionary dating rarely works. It's much more likely that the non-Christian will pull the Christian in the wrong direction. The fact is, the non-Christian doesn't have a new nature from Christ, so he or she will not be naturally drawn in your direction as a Christ follower. On the other hand, Christians do have an old nature and can easily find themselves drawn in *that* direction. You might say that gravity will be working against you as a Christian dating a non-Christian rather than the other way around. Far too many of these "friendships" turn into sexual relationships, and you find yourself trapped in a liaison that will hurt you, drag you down, and eventually break your heart.

Is your prospective boyfriend or girlfriend an authentic believer in Christ, a sincere follower of Jesus who walks the walk as well as talks the talk? There are people who may be technically saved but have never grown in Christ. Instead, they are immature believers and are frequently ruled by their old nature.

Here is what you ought to ask yourself: *After spending time with this person, do they build me up or tear me down? After I have been with this individual for the evening, how do I feel afterward? Do I feel encouraged in my faith and my walk with the Lord? Did we really have fun together, or was it kind of a drag? Did I feel as though this person was making me uncomfortable and pushing me toward compromise?*

You want to find a real Christian as a potential mate. But don't stop there! More than just finding a Christian person, you need to find a *godly* person—someone who truly loves Jesus and walks daily with Him.

In 2 Timothy 2:22, Paul told his young friend Timothy, "Run from anything that stimulates youthful lusts. Instead, pursue righteous living, faithfulness, love, and peace. Enjoy the companionship of those who call on the Lord with pure hearts" (NLT).

Here is a simple way to sum it up: Find someone more godly than you. Find someone who is actually stronger than you, to whom you can look up to and admire. Then, having established that the individual would be a good potential mate, don't rush the process. Give time for the relationship to deepen and mature. If your love is genuine, it will stand the test of time.

A DEEPER LOOK AT LOVE

"Love Is Patient"

How do you know if you're in love? In one of the most beautiful chapters in all of Scripture, the apostle Paul took time to describe both what love is and what it is not:

> Love is patient and kind. Love is not jealous or boastful or proud or rude. It does not demand its own way. It is not irritable, and it keeps no record of being wronged. It does not rejoice about injustice but rejoices

> whenever the truth wins out. Love never gives up, never loses faith, is always hopeful, and endures through every circumstance. (1 Corinthians 13:4-7, NLT)

When Paul says that love is *patient*, the word could be translated as "long-tempered" (as compared with short-tempered). The word used here is common in the New Testament and speaks almost exclusively of being patient with people rather than with circumstances or events.

If you meet someone you are attracted to and think there might be potential in the relationship, don't make that person your project and keep telling yourself, *I'm going to change her*. Chances are that you won't. And the quality that you don't like may get worse before it gets any better. If you can't love that individual just as he or she is, that is a good sign this might not be the right person for you.

Love is patient. You have to be patient with people. And if your love is genuine, it will truly last. Song of Solomon 8:7 says, "Many waters cannot quench love; rivers cannot wash it away" (NIV). Better to sort these things out before tying the knot. Breaking up is better than divorce. Breaking an engagement is better than divorce. Even walking out on your wedding, right in the middle of the ceremony, is better than divorce.

Be patient and give love time to grow.

In the Bible, we read that Jacob worked seven years for Laban for the privilege of marrying his daughter Rachel. The Bible tells us, "Jacob worked seven years to pay for Rachel. But his love for her was so strong that it seemed to him but a few days" (Genesis 29:20, NLT).

If you're saying, *Oh, we just can't wait*, then maybe it

isn't love; maybe it's lust. If it's truly love, it will stand the test of time. Love is patient.

What Do We Mean by "Love"?

In English, we have one word for love, and we use it for just about everything. *I love my car. I love my dog. I love that movie. I love enchiladas. I love my girlfriend or boyfriend.* However, in the language of the New Testament, there are several words for love. The Greek word *eros* is mainly physical attraction, or the sexual aspect of love. *Phileo* speaks of brotherly love, family love, or the love between friends. The word most commonly translated as "love" in the New Testament is the word *agape*, which speaks of the highest form of self-giving love. Everything we read in 1 Corinthians 13 was a definition of *agape*. In John 3:16, where we read, "For God so loved the world," it uses the word *agape*. When the Bible tells us that "God is love," it once again uses *agape*. It's the same with the verse that says, "Greater love has no one than this, than to lay down one's life for his friends" (John 15:13).

Every one of these loves has its place in a relationship. *Eros* speaks of physical and sexual attraction, which is just fine in the right place and the right time. If *eros* is in marriage where it can be righteously fulfilled, it is a *good* thing to be sexually attracted to your spouse. Prior to marriage, *eros* is what attracts you to a person of the opposite sex so that you notice him or her: "What a great-looking guy" or "Wow, look at that girl!" In other words, *eros* is part of the magnetism that brings a man and woman together in a relationship.

Phileo speaks of the love between friends. To contrast, *eros* wants something from someone. *Phileo* is a giving love but still expects something in return. *Agape*, however, will give, wanting nothing in return.

If we compared it to gift giving, *eros* would say, "I just want the gift from you right now." *Phileo* would say, "I will give you a gift, but what are you giving me in return?" But *agape* would say, "Here is a gift you could never pay for ever, but I am giving it to you because I love you."

Tragically, many relationships are built on *eros* today.

She once was hot, but now that she is no longer hot, you dump her.

He used to have plenty of money, but now that he's out of a job, well, he's a loser, and you get rid of him.

As a result, people tend to drift from relationship to relationship, telling others how they "fall in" and "out of" love. The fact is, they never were really in love at all—not with the kind of genuine, lasting love that will go the distance. There is a place for *eros* love and *phileo* love in a marriage, but you want to build on a foundation of *agape* love—the love that gives and gives, endures and endures.

SEX AND SINGLENESS

What the Bible says about sex and the single person can be summed up in a word: no.

Should I spell that out?

N-O.

Greg, are you saying that a single person can't have sex?

Exactly. More important, that is what God is saying.

Obviously, sex is not bad; it is good. We wouldn't be here without sex. But it has been created by God to be enjoyed within a marriage relationship between a husband

and wife. Sex outside of marriage is never the will of God.

Someone will say, "Well, Greg, that's your interpretation, and I think your interpretation is very narrow. My god is loving, and my god wants me to express myself. My god says it's okay to have sex with my significant other."

I actually don't dispute that. I simply would caution you not to mix your god up with the God of the Bible. You have another god, and you can follow that other god all you like. Just don't expect that god to save you or take you to heaven.

Here is what the true and living God, the God of the Bible, says about sex: "It is God's will that you should be sanctified [set apart]: that you should avoid sexual immorality" (1 Thessalonians 4:3, NIV).

Hebrews 13:4 says, "Give honor to marriage, and remain faithful to one another in marriage. God will surely judge people who are immoral and those who commit adultery" (NLT).

Then Proverbs 5:15-17 adds, "Drink water from your own well—share your love only with your wife. Why spill the water of your springs in the streets, having sex with just anyone? You should reserve it for yourselves. Never share it with strangers" (NLT).

A rushing river within its banks is a thing of beauty and does so many helpful and wonderful things. But when that same stream goes out of its banks, it becomes something destructive, bringing ruin and heartache. In the same way, sex within its proper context is a powerful force for good, just as God intended. Outside of marriage, however, it becomes unbelievably harmful to the mind, the soul, and even the body.

That's why there is no such thing as a one-night fling.

You might say, "Oh, it didn't mean anything." But it *does*. It means a great deal. Why? Because when you enter into a sexual union with someone, you effectively become one flesh with that person. And, by the way, that even applies to a guy who hires a prostitute for the night—or a woman who does the same. The apostle Paul was very clear on this in his first letter to the church in Corinth:

> Don't you realize that your bodies are actually parts of Christ? Should a man take his body, which is part of Christ, and join it to a prostitute? Never! And don't you know that if a man joins himself to a prostitute, he becomes one body with her? For the Scriptures say, "The two are united into one." But the person who is joined to the Lord is one spirit with him.
>
> Run from sexual sin! No other sin so clearly affects the body as this one does. For sexual immorality is a sin against your own body. Don't you realize that your body is the temple of the Holy Spirit, who lives in you and was given to you by God? You do not belong to yourself, for God bought you with a high price. So you must honor God with your body. (I Corinthians 6:15-20, NLT)

You say, "It's okay, Greg, we're practicing safe sex."

No, you need to *save* sex—for marriage. You need to make this decision to remain pure in the front seat of the church, not in the backseat of your car. Decide now. Don't decide later, when the lights are down, the temptation is high, and the music is playing. (And have you noticed? It seems like it's always a saxophone! When something seductive or weird is about to happen in a movie, the saxophone starts playing.)

Someone says to me, "Come on, Greg. This doesn't hurt anyone."

Really? Have you ever heard of AIDS? AIDS is the leading killer of Americans between the ages twenty-five and forty-four. So, is the answer "safe sex"? No. The answer is *abstinence*.

You say that sex outside of marriage doesn't *hurt* anyone? What about an unplanned pregnancy?

"Well, Greg, we'll just deal with that if we have to. We will abort the fetus."

Oh, is that what you call it? I call it murdering an unborn child. The Bible recognizes a preborn baby as a human being (see Jeremiah 1:5-6; Psalm 139:15-16). The full ramifications of aborting a baby may not hit you until much later in life, when you realize that you have killed an innocent child simply because you didn't want to be inconvenienced.

I thank God that my mom didn't abort me. I was conceived out of wedlock and wasn't "planned," but God has a plan for every child. There are no illegitimate children, only illegitimate parents. Every child deserves to live.

So any man or woman who asks you to prove your love by having sex is a loser. I would put the brakes on that relationship right there.

The Bible tells the story of Samson, whose entire life was devastated by sexual sin because he thought he could handle it. And the reason he thought he could handle it was because he was such a physically powerful man and had destroyed so many of Israel's enemies. On one occasion, he destroyed a thousand Philistines with the jawbone of a donkey he had picked up from the ground. He was strong enough to tear down a city's gates and carry them on his back. The Bible says he performed feats of great strength when the Spirit of God came on him. And because he was so fearsome on the battlefield, he thought he could handle anything in life.

But Satan knew Samson's Achilles' heel. He was a he-man with a she weakness. So the devil didn't take him down on the battlefield or fighting against an army; he took him down in the bedroom, with a girl named Delilah.

Contrast Samson with Joseph in the book of Genesis. The Bible tells us Joseph was a handsome young man. He certainly must have had a normal sex drive. He was working for a wealthy, powerful man named Potiphar in the land of Egypt. Potiphar had a wife who most likely was attractive. She was also bored and spent much of her time scheming on how to seduce the young servant.

Again and again she propositioned him, and I'm sure she had ways of making herself very attractive and tempting to a healthy young man. Again and again, however, Joseph refused. He wouldn't betray his master, Potiphar, and he wouldn't sin against God.

Scripture records it like this:

> He said to his master's wife, "Look, with me here, my master doesn't give a second thought to anything that goes on here — he's put me in charge of everything he owns. He treats me as an equal. The only thing he hasn't turned over to me is you. You're his wife, after all! How could I violate his trust and sin against God?"
>
> She pestered him day after day after day, but he stood his ground. He refused to go to bed with her. (Genesis 39:8-10, MSG)

And then came the day when Mrs. Potiphar turned into a full predator:

> On one of these days he came to the house to do his work and none of the household servants happened to be there. She grabbed him by his cloak, saying, "Sleep with me!" He left his coat in her hand and ran out of the house. (verse 11, MSG)

How do you deal with sexual temptation? Don't dally with it, as Samson did, telling yourself that you can play around the edges with sex and not get burned. No, do what Joseph did: Run. Sometimes it is literally as simple as that.

Get out of that situation—even if it's awkward, even if it's humiliating, even if you leave something behind. Just drop everything and run. There is always a way out:

> No temptation has seized you except what is common to man. And God is faithful; he will not let you be tempted beyond what you can bear. But when you are tempted, he will also provide a way out so that you can stand up under it. (1 Corinthians 10:13, NIV)

In other words, God will never give you more than you can handle, and there is always a way out. Sometimes the way out is as simple as a door. Use it! Flee temptation and don't leave a forwarding address.

You might say, "I guess it's too late for me, Greg. I've already fallen. I'm already living with my significant other." Or maybe, "I've already had an abortion, and I feel pretty guilty about it. What should I do?"

Here is what you need to do. Confess these things to God for what they are: sin against Him. Call it what it is, and ask for His forgiveness. And guess what? He will forgive you.

Remember the woman in John 8 who had been caught in the very act of adultery? She was surrounded by her accusers, each with a rock in his hand, ready to stone her to death. They had dumped her at Jesus' feet to see how He would deal with her. And what did He do? He got rid of her accusers, and then He turned to her and said,

> "Where are those accusers of yours? Has no one condemned you?"
>
> She said, "No one, Lord."
>
> And Jesus said to her, "Neither do I condemn you; go and sin no more." (verses 10-11)

If you tell God you are sorry for your sin and repent —change your behavior—He will forgive you. If you are living with someone outside of marriage, you change the situation and move out. If you are having sex with someone who isn't your spouse, you stop doing so. If you are looking at pornography, you get rid of it and stay completely away from it. Get rid of your computer if you need to. Do whatever you need to do and take whatever measures you need to take to put up the proper barriers in your life.

If you find yourself in a relationship in which you are feeling weak and compromised, you probably need a new relationship. Make the appropriate changes and you will see things improve quickly. If you have conceived a child out of wedlock, carry that baby to term. If you don't feel you can raise the child, put him or her up for adoption. There are wonderful Christian agencies that will adopt that child out to a loving family who will raise that little one in the way of the Lord.

Take the appropriate measures. And as Jesus said, "Go and sin no more."

CHAPTER FOUR

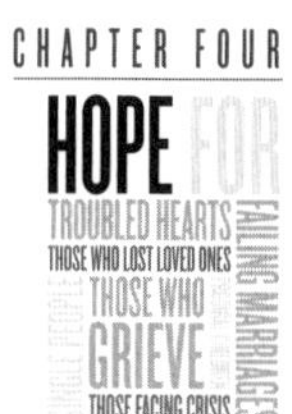

HOPE FOR HURTING MARRIAGES

PART I

A PASTOR WAS INVITED to speak to a group of fourth graders on the topic of marriage. As the children took their seats in the little wooden chairs, the preacher smiled and said, "Kids, I want to talk to you about marriage today. I wonder if any of you could tell me what God has to say about marriage."

Immediately one little boy waved his hand back and forth, so the pastor called on him. "Okay, son," he said, "what does God say about marriage?"

The boy replied, "Father, forgive them, for they know not what they do."

There are a lot of miserable people out there who have not found their marriages to be what they had expected. Maybe that is why one disillusioned soul wrote, "Marriage is like a three-ring circus: engagement ring, wedding ring, and suffering."

Oscar Wilde said, "The world has grown suspicious of anything that looks like a happily married life."

Oil tycoon J. Paul Getty, one of the richest men who ever lived, said, "I would gladly give all my millions for just one lasting marital success."

IS A HAPPY MARRIAGE EVEN POSSIBLE?

Can a man and a woman fall in love, like they do in the fairy tales, and live "happily ever after"? One has to wonder, given the divorce rate today. It's somewhere around 50 percent, and it continues to rise. The fact is, the more times you are married, the higher the percentage is that you will eventually divorce. The divorce rate for second marriages is at 60 percent. And for a third marriage, it rises even higher, to 73 percent.

Maybe, even as you are reading this chapter right now, your marriage is in real trouble. It is hanging by a thread, and the thread is on fire. Perhaps you are even considering divorce and you've all but given up. I want to offer you a strong word of hope from the Bible. Is it possible to have a happy and fulfilling marriage? Yes, it is! It can be done, as my wife, Cathe, and I have experienced, and I want you to experience that as well.

Now, don't get me wrong. I'm not suggesting that you and your spouse won't face problems or challenges. Every married couple comes under pressures, difficulties, and hardships. But I do believe that it is possible to have a very fulfilling marriage—if you go about it the right way. I think I can speak with some experience on the topic of marriage and divorce, for three reasons.

First, I have been up close and personal with divorce. Although I have never been divorced myself, my mother was married and divorced seven times. Don't tell me it doesn't affect the kids. Anyone who says something like that has never had parents who divorced. I know how it affected me. It was devastating. I have seen what divorce can do, and that fact created a great determination within me to find the right girl and build a successful marriage and home.

The second reason I think I can address this topic is because I have been married now for thirty-eight years. Cathe and I are thankful to God for that and give Him the glory.

A third reason I can speak to this topic is because I have been counseling people with marital difficulties for almost forty years now and have pretty much heard and seen it all.

It's my firm belief that most of the divorces I have witnessed through my years of ministry never needed to happen; those marriages could have been saved. I have seen marriages in the worst shape imaginable get put back together with God's grace and strong help. He's still the God of miracles!

When a couple comes to me for counseling, often I will ask them a few questions. I will start with "Are you both Christians?" Almost always they will say, "Oh, yes, we're Christians, and that's why we're here to see you."

Then I will ask them, "Do you believe that the Bible is the Word of God?"

Again, couples will reply, "Yes, we do. We love the Bible."

Then I will ask them a third question: "Are you willing to do what the Bible says, even if you find it difficult?"

At that point, they know they're in trouble. They want

to say yes, but they're afraid of what comes next—what I might ask them to do. If they can't answer yes to all three of those questions, our conversation is effectively over. If they're unwilling to obey God's Word and follow God's plans and counsel, I frankly don't know how to help them.

The fact is, we need to think biblically about marriage instead of taking our cues from contemporary culture. What does our culture know about marriage? What does Hollywood know about marriage? These people can't keep any relationship together. We need a much more authoritative source on something so crucial and central to our lives, and that source is the Word of God. We need God's help—more than ever.

CHECKING OUT YOUR FOUNDATION

Cathe and I courted for three years prior to getting married. We loved each other, but, frankly, we argued quite a bit and broke up three times. I'm talking big breakups here, as in "I never want to see you again."

But the breakups never lasted very long, and as time went by, I realized just how much I loved this woman. As the Bible says, "Many waters cannot quench love, nor can the floods drown it" (Song of Solomon 8:7). I recognized that this love for Cathe was real and that it was from God because it grew stronger with the passing of time.

Dr. James Dobson once said, "Don't marry the person you think you can live with; marry only the individual you think you can't live without." After three years, Cathe and I decided we couldn't live without each other.

Our marriage has been tested, just like every marriage will be tested, and we have weathered some mighty storms together. The most devastating storm was when our son died. Many marriages don't survive that kind of blow, but we looked to the Lord. He has gotten us through it, and He is *getting* us through it.

Every marriage, however, will face pressures and hardships and come under attack. The question is, are you building your relationship on a strong foundation? As He was wrapping up His Sermon on the Mount, Jesus said these words:

> Anyone who listens to my teaching and follows it is wise, like a person who builds a house on solid rock. Though the rain comes in torrents and the floodwaters rise and the winds beat against that house, it won't collapse because it is built on bedrock. But anyone who hears my teaching and doesn't obey it is foolish, like a person who builds a house on sand. When the rains and floods come and the winds beat against that house, it will collapse with a mighty crash. (Matthew 7:24-27, NLT)

So here is my question for you: Is your marriage built on the rock, or is it on the rocks? Have you ever built a sandcastle on the beach? You can invest hours and hours on the project, adding a moat and all the little towers and turrets. Then a wave comes along, and it's gone! That is what happens to marriages built on sand; they won't survive the storm and might not make it past the first wave. A marriage built on the rock not only will survive the storm but will actually get stronger through those dark and windy days.

Notice that Jesus didn't say, "*If* the rains and floods come" but rather "*When* the rains and floods come." Every marriage will experience storms.

Sometimes (just to get a reaction) I will tell people that I've been married to five different women, all named Cathe and spelled the same way. Why do I say that? Because the woman I am married to today is not the same woman I married back in 1974. And I'm not the same man she married either. The Cathe of age thirty was not the same as the Cathe of age eighteen. And the Cathe of age forty was not at all the same as the Cathe aged thirty. The point is, people change through the passing of time. In my case, I'm happy to tell you that every new Cathe has been better than the last one. (But they were all good.)

Every marriage will go through changes, and every marriage will be tested. That's why it's so important to have a solid foundation that can endure any storm and will give stability to a marriage through the years. We want to build our marriages on the foundation of Christ Himself.

The Bible says, "He who finds a wife finds what is good and receives favor from the LORD" (Proverbs 18:22, NIV). Amen to that. I have found that a good marriage halves our sorrows, doubles our joys, and quadruples our expenses! But it's all good.

Here's what it comes down to. One day when your life is almost over, there really will be only three things that matter to you: your faith, your family, and, to a lesser degree, your friends. Believe me, you won't lie there on your deathbed and fret about your business, your investments, or your 401k. All that stuff will be in the rearview mirror, almost out of sight. What you will be thinking about is God and your family. In far too many cases, I've been with dying people who are filled with regret that they didn't walk with God in their lives and didn't treat their families the way they should have.

So instead of waiting for that day, why not deal with it now? Why not honor your marriage commitment and avoid the sorrow of looking back on broken relationships and broken lives?

There have been many times when I've wished we could strike the very word *divorce* from our vocabularies. It is brought up far too quickly, easily, and casually. Wedlock should be a padlock. As I mentioned before, if a given marriage is miserable and unhappy, the fault lies with the participants, not the institution.

WHAT THE BIBLE SAYS ABOUT DIVORCE

While the Bible does allow for divorce in certain cases, I can tell you that legitimate biblical divorces are very rare. Most divorces I have seen come down to a husband and wife who have allowed themselves to sink into a cycle of selfishness. And I have also seen the regret many of these people feel—months and even years later—that they hadn't given more priority and attention to their marriage while they still had a chance.

This isn't just a pastor talking. Even people in our non-Christian culture recognize the devastating effects of divorce. Not long ago, I read an article by a Hollywood screenwriter named Gigi Levangie Grazer in *The Huffington Post*. I'll tip you off in advance that she loves the word *sucks*, but what we want here is a viewpoint from someone within our contemporary world.

She wrote,

> Divorce sucks.
>
> I mean, it really sucks. Got kids? If so, don't do it.
>
> You probably think you have no reason to listen to me. . . . But, hey, I've lived a pretty long time — by L.A. standards, I'm ancient — and I've had many life experiences, among them two marriages. . . .
>
> What I've learned since is that divorce lingers. It makes you sad when you least expect it. It colors everything. . . . And you can tell yourself, Yeah, I did it for my kids, so they could grow up with a healthy mother, a happier mother who had more time for them. But single motherhood, even with access to help, is not for sissies.[1]

She went on to cite further reasons for not getting divorced.

That article reminds me of a story I once read. A woman went to see a lawyer, telling him, "I want to divorce my husband. I hate him, and I want to hurt him. So give me some advice."

The attorney thought about it for a moment and said, "I have an idea. You're going to divorce the guy, right? Okay, here's what I would suggest to you. For three months, don't criticize him. In fact, speak only well of him. Build him up. Tell him how wonderful he is. Tell him how much you love him. Every time he does something nice, commend him for it. Tell him what a great guy he is for the next three months. And after he thinks he has your confidence, then just say, 'I'm going to divorce you.' It will hurt even worse!"

The woman thought that sounded like a good idea, so that is what she did for the next three months. She affirmed her husband, told him how much she loved him, and built him up in every way she could. When the time was up, the lawyer called her and said, "Okay, let's get started."

"Oh, no," she replied. "We're going on a second honeymoon!"

She had changed her behavior, and it turned their relationship around.

Having a successful marriage doesn't happen by accident. It is not unlike your relationship with Christ. Though you become a Christian when you put your faith in Jesus, your *walk* with the Lord is developed through daily commitment, prayer, and Bible study—in short, through dedicated effort on your part. The same is true of a marriage. The moment you begin to neglect a marriage, it will start unraveling. Please take my word on this: You need to be doing everything you can to keep your marriage strong, not taking it for granted even one moment.

Let's read what Jesus said to those who had lost hope for their hurting marriages. Remember, what He said was designed to restore hope again:

> The Pharisees also came to Him, testing Him, and saying to Him, "Is it lawful for a man to divorce his wife for just any reason?"
>
> And He answered and said to them, "Have you not read that He who made them at the beginning 'made them male and female,' and said, 'For this reason a man shall leave his father and mother and be joined to his wife, and the two shall become one flesh'? So then, they are no longer two but one flesh. Therefore what God has joined together, let not man separate." (Matthew 19:3-6)

Jesus declined to answer their direct question but instead took them all the way back to the Garden of Eden and God's original plan. In other words, instead of providing them with a convenient exit from marriage, He pointed them to the way to stay married.

It's logical that He would do this, because He was there, as Creator, in that long-ago garden. No one could know better how God had intended the husband-wife relationship to work than the One who invented it in the first place.

Adam, of course, had the ultimate setup, the best bachelor pad ever. He had all the delicious food he wanted to eat, meaningful work and responsibility, the whole wild and entertaining animal kingdom for companionship, and, of course, the daily fellowship of the Lord Himself.

As time went by, however, and Adam noted the males and females of all the species and how they always walked together, sharing their food, their nests and dens, and how they brought up their little families, he must have felt something missing.

Was it an ache? An empty place? Or was it just an inner, deep-down knowledge that his life wasn't complete?

God looked at Adam and basically said, "Not good is the aloneness of man" (See Genesis 2:18). And so the Lord caused a deep sleep to fall upon Adam, and He created Eve and brought her to the man's side.

Also in Genesis 2:18, God said, "I will make him a helper comparable to him." From the Hebrew, that could be translated, "I will make someone who assists another to reach fulfillment." It is also translated "someone who comes to rescue another." Eve would provide what was missing in Adam's life.

LEAVE AND CLEAVE

In His response to the Pharisees, Jesus used two operative words that make for a successful and happy marriage: *leave* and *cleave.* A lasting, successful, and happy marriage—according to Jesus Himself—begins with the leaving. In effect, you are leaving all other relationships.

The Lord speaks here of the closest relationship outside of marriage: that of a son to his parents. He says, "A man shall leave his father and mother" (Matthew 19:5). Now, that doesn't mean the man is no longer a son to his mom and dad, but it does mean the dynamics of that relationship have now changed. That man's responsibility as a son has been superseded by his responsibility as a husband, ultimately as a father, and as the head of his own home. He still must honor his parents, but a clear and definitive leaving must take place.

Sometimes guys just don't get this. Instead of stepping up as men in their own families, they continually try to please their mothers and fathers.

Leaving means giving every other relationship in life a lesser degree of importance. That means that when you get married, your best friend should be your spouse. Yes, you can still have those other relationships, but they must always take a backseat to your primary relationship with your spouse.

In Malachi 2:14, we read, "The LORD is acting as the witness between you and the wife of your youth, because you have broken faith with her, though she is your partner, the wife of your marriage covenant" (NIV).

Partner and wife. It doesn't just say she is your wife. She is your partner, the one with whom you are united in thoughts, goals, plans, and efforts.

Does that describe you as a husband or wife? How well do you know your spouse? Do you know what he or she really cares about? What your spouse likes to do? His or her favorite food? Favorite color? How well do you really know one another? If you don't treat your wife as you ought to as a husband, it actually could bring your prayer life to a screeching halt. In 1 Peter 3:7, the Bible says this: "Husbands, likewise, dwell with them with understanding, giving honor to the wife, as to the weaker vessel, and as being heirs together of the grace of life, that your prayers may not be hindered."

The text is saying here that your prayers *will* be hindered if your marriage is out of whack. Aside from our relationship with Him, God wants us to make our marriage the number one priority in life.

By the way, the word used in the above verse for *dwell* doesn't just mean "live with her." It's more than that. It actually could be translated "be aligned to her," or even "give maintenance to her." We maintain things in life that we value, don't we? We maintain our homes and our cars, our motorcycles and RVs. What happens if you have a car and you never do anything for it? You never change the oil or even put air in the tires if they go flat. You just keep on driving and driving. You'll eventually grind to a stop, won't you? Your car will break down. And the same happens in a marriage if you don't maintain it. If you aren't attentive and take care of this most important human relationship, it will soon break down.

I'm always impressed when I see a classic car drive by with a really old person driving it. I conclude that it probably was their car in the beginning and they have maintained it and lavished care on it through the years.

That is the way you want your marriage to be. You don't want to trade him or her in for a new model. You want to tenderly care for your marriage, turning it into a classic that will stand the test of time.

This may mean asking yourself an important question every now and then: *Is there any relationship or pursuit I am involved in that would put distance between me and my mate?*

Believe it or not, I've learned to listen to my wife and heed the things she says to me. And if she were to say that she thought I was spending too much time doing thus and so or hanging around with a certain person, I would listen to that and make some changes. And she would do the same if I said something similar to her. What you do with your time *is* your spouse's business because he or she is your partner and companion.

Maybe you're involved in some activity or pursuit and have become excited and passionate about it—it even could be a worthy cause—but it's beginning to cut into the time you have with your spouse and taking you away from home more often and for longer periods of time. You have to be willing to ask yourself, *Is this thing hurting or helping my marriage?*

The emphasis in Scripture, by the way, is always on the husband. Notice that Peter told husbands to "dwell with [your wives] with understanding" (1 Peter 3:7). Of course, it would be helpful if wives used some wisdom and understanding in living with their husbands as well, but that isn't the emphasis of Scripture. God puts the onus on husbands to take the lead in the marriage relationship. When Paul spoke about marriage, he said, “Husbands, love your wives, just as Christ loved the church and gave himself up for her” (Ephesians 5:25, NIV).

Again, husbands are to step up, and husbands are to take the lead. Why? Because if a husband is doing what he ought to be doing, in most cases the wife will respond appropriately. Treat your wife like a thoroughbred and she will never become a nag. Let her know that you love her. Be the spiritual leader in your home and the one who initiates these plans to improve your marriage.

Why do we love God right now? The Bible says, “We love Him because He first loved us” (1 John 4:19). In other words, our love is a response to His love. And the same is true in a marriage. Husband, your wife will respond and do what God wants her to do if you do your part. So don’t tell me about your wife’s not doing her part. Don’t you worry about that. It is between her and the Lord. You just make sure you’re doing your part as a loving leader in the marriage.

We spoke about how a husband and wife must leave their parents and every other relationship in order to cleave to each other and become one flesh. It’s really not much use leaving unless you spend a lifetime cleaving.

What does it mean to cleave? It means to adhere or stick to something or to become attached by some strong tie. And, by the way, that doesn’t mean you’re stuck together against your will. It means you are holding on to one another. In fact, in the original language, *cleave* speaks of a determined effort.

Think of it this way. You are climbing up the side of the cliff. Are you stuck to that cliff face, or are you holding on? You’re holding on! Why? Because you want to live. And that is how you keep a marriage strong as well.

When we see the word used again in the New Testament, it is translated "to be cemented together." In other words, to stick like glue, to be welded together so tightly that the two of you can't be separated without doing serious damage to both.

Have you ever used Super Glue? I was always a really lousy model builder, but I kept trying. When I was a kid, I would get glue all over everything. I never seemed to have enough patience to let the glue dry before I painted. No, I would start painting before the glue had a chance to bond. So I ended up making a mess, with glue adhering to my fingertips like a second set of prints.

The idea being conveyed in Scripture is to stick together as though you were Super-Glued. You are one person and one flesh.

COMMUNICATION

Being one person and one flesh means you must have constant communication. This is one of the keys to a successful marriage. I've heard it said that there are two times when a man doesn't understand a woman: before marriage and after marriage. That's a joke, of course, but it's true that we have to work at communicating with each other and understanding each other. And this means you have to learn how to disagree agreeably.

Sometimes I will have a man and woman who want to get married come to my office to see me, and they will go on and on, telling me how much they love each other. I will say, "Have you two ever had a disagreement? An argument?"

"Oh, no. We love each other too much. He is so sweet."

"And she is so gorgeous."

"So you've never had a fight?" I ask them.

"No. And we never plan on having one."

"Okay," I will say, "the interview is over. You can leave now. Come back to see me after you've entered the real world." Why do I say that? Because the simple fact is, you will have many disagreements in life, so you had better learn how to fight fair. You had better learn how to disagree agreeably. It will require you to bend, compromise, and forgive, forgive, forgive.

Ruth Graham once said that a good marriage consists of two good forgivers. That is true. If you aren't a good forgiver, then you're not going to have a good marriage.

In addition to forgiving each other, you need to affirm one another. Husbands, when is the last time you hugged your wife without ulterior motives, hoping it would lead to something? Wives, when is the last time you told your husband how much you appreciated him?

I honestly believe most divorces could be averted if we would just start with the operative principles of leaving and cleaving. It would make all the difference in the world because marriage isn't so much *finding* the right person as it is *being* the right person. That means going into marriage asking yourself, *How can I fulfill this person's needs?*

This may come as a shock, but marriage is not about *you.*

If you are intending to marry someone so that he or she can meet all your needs and make you happy, then you had better not go through with it. Laying all your hopes and expectations on your spouse is a way to sink the boat—very fast. If, on the other hand, you can put the needs of your mate above your own, you will see dramatic things take place.

In fact, the Bible tells us in Ephesians 5—*before* the wife is told to submit to her husband—that husbands and wives are to submit one to another in the fear of God.

Some people choke a little on the word *submit.* The truth is, you and I have to submit all the time. If you're driving down the street and see a car with lights flashing behind you, you submit real fast. That is because we live by rules and standards and recognize there are people who are in authority over our lives.

Most of us have a boss at work and submit to his or her instructions. Maybe you're in school and your teacher gives you a specific assignment. You submit to those instructions if you want to achieve a passing grade on that paper.

We all submit, and there is nothing wrong with that. It's a *good* thing. What specifically, though, does it mean for a wife to submit to her husband? Maybe we need to come up with a different word here, because many people think that submitting means giving up all our rights and being a doormat or a victim or taking whatever someone dishes out to us.

Actually the word *submit* could be better translated "to order oneself under" someone. In the military sense, it means to rank beneath, or rank under. So a husband's submission to his wife does not mean that he abdicates his responsibility of leadership in the home. It means he helps her to bear her burdens. He gets underneath her to carry her cares.

Imagine that my wife comes home from the grocery store with a trunk full of groceries. As she begins unloading them and bringing them in the house, bag after bag, I just sit there and watch her. And then I ask, "When will dinner be ready?"

No, I would never do that! I immediately jump up and help her carry those bags, and usually I grab the heaviest ones. Why? Because I love her and want to assist her. I "submit" to her in that, gladly, because I want to carry the heavy loads for her.

When we're speaking of life in general, a wife will say, "I want to do all I can to help you become the man God has called you to be."

And the husband will say, "I want to make every effort to help you become all God has planned for you and desires for you."

We say to one another, "I'm your number one fan. I'm your cheerleader. I'm in your corner. You can depend on me, and I'm always here for you."

What a difference that makes in life when we submit our own needs and wants to the needs and wants of our mates and when we constantly hold one another up.

Do you know how much God hates divorce? Here is what he said in Malachi 2:16: " 'I hate divorce!' says the LORD, the God of Israel. 'To divorce your wife is to overwhelm her with cruelty,' says the LORD of Heaven's Armies. 'So guard your heart; do not be unfaithful to your wife' " (NLT).

A different translation puts it like this: "I hate the violent dismembering of the 'one flesh' of marriage" (MSG). In other words, there's no such thing as "a clean divorce." In God's eyes, it's a messy, even bloody thing, like the tearing of flesh.

For those who are already divorced, I don't say these things to put you under condemnation. What's done is done. If you have been divorced and remarried, then this is the time to get it right. With all my heart, I believe in a forgiving God and a God of second chances. But don't repeat the same behavior that tore up your first marriage. We need to learn from our experiences and, more important, learn from the Word of God.

Back in Matthew 19, where Jesus was confronting the Pharisees over this issue, we see that even though Jesus had talked to them about marriage, they still wanted to haggle over the issue of divorce:

> They said to Him, "Why then did Moses command to give a certificate of divorce, and to put her away?"
>
> He said to them, "Moses, because of the hardness of your hearts, permitted you to divorce your wives, but from the beginning it was not so. And I say to you, whoever divorces his wife, except for sexual immorality, and marries another, commits adultery; and whoever marries her who is divorced commits adultery." (verses 7-9)

Notice how the Pharisees said, "Why then did Moses *command* divorce?" But Jesus corrected them, essentially saying, "He didn't command it. He *permitted* it. You have it wrong."

It might surprise you to learn that attitudes toward marriage were very liberal back in those days. Divorce was widespread in Israel. Remember the Samaritan woman Jesus spoke to at the well in Sychar (see John 4)? She had been married and divorced five times. So it was actually quite commonplace. Hillel, a liberal rabbi of the day, said that even incompatibility of temperament was grounds for divorce. In that culture, a man could divorce his wife for such trivial things as burning his meal or embarrassing him in front of his friends. For that matter, he could divorce her if he became tired of her and a more attractive woman came along.

Our modern equivalent to this would be the term *irreconcilable differences.* You hear those words being tossed around all the time.

"Our marriage didn't work out."

"Why?"

"Irreconcilable differences."

Really? I've had irreconcilable differences with my wife for thirty-eight years now. She's neat, and I'm messy. She is sometimes late, and I'm usually early to everything. She's cute, and me? Well, not so much. What are we going to do with those "irreconcilable differences"? Get divorced? Not a chance! No, we're going to work things out, we're going to flex, we're going to keep on adapting to each other, and we're going to put the needs of each other above our own.

Listen, *every* marriage will have irreconcilable differences. Just being a man joined to a woman is an irreconcilable difference, so that is not a biblical allowance for divorce.

Jesus, however, did make an allowance for divorce in a couple of specific situations.

BIBLICAL GROUNDS FOR DIVORCE

Sexual Immorality

> I say to you, whoever divorces his wife, except for sexual immorality, and marries another, commits adultery. (Matthew 19:9)

The term *sexual immorality* comes from the Greek word *pornea*, from which we get our English word *pornography.* Sexual immorality encompasses multiple behaviors, including adultery, incest, prostitution, and homosexuality.

Why is this such a deal breaker? Why would God permit something as drastic as a divorce because of this? It's because when you have sex with someone, you actually become one flesh with that person. Paul even said that if you have sexual relations with a prostitute, you become one flesh with her (see 1 Corinthians 6:16). So don't tell me, "It really didn't mean anything" or "It was just a one-night stand."

It might not have meant much to you, but it meant a great deal to God. And He tells us in His Word that we can't treat sex in that way. A sexual union is a very sacred union in God's sight. As a result, when you break that union with your spouse and join yourself sexually to someone else, you have violated something very significant in His sight.

Unfaithfulness is grounds for divorce.

But unfaithfulness is also grounds for forgiveness, and I have seen many marriages survive even this devastating trial. I could tell you story after story of couples who have decided on forgiveness and rebuilding trust and love in their marriage, and they have been very glad they did.

Yes, unfaithfulness is biblical grounds for divorce, so don't go down that road. Don't even play with it in your mind, spinning fantasies and lustful imaginations. Why? Because the first step to doing it is thinking about it.

Love your wife. Love your husband. Be loyal and faithful to your God-given companion because the road of deceit and adultery leads to inexpressible pain. And after you pay the price, your kids will have to pay the price, and it will be an extremely difficult price for them to pay.

Desertion

Scripture gives one more situation in which God will allow for a divorce:

> If a Christian man has a wife who is not a believer and she is willing to continue living with him, he must not leave her. And if a Christian woman has a husband who is not a believer, and he is willing to continue living with her, she must not leave him. . . . (But if the husband or wife who isn't a believer insists on leaving, let them go. In such cases the Christian husband or wife is no longer bound to the other, for God has called you to live in peace.) Don't you wives must realize that your husbands might be saved because of you? And don't you husbands must realize that your wives might be saved because of you? (1 Corinthians 7:12-13,15-16, NLT)

In the New King James Version, we read, "If the unbeliever departs, let him depart; a brother or a sister is not under bondage in such cases" (verse 15).

Let's say you are a woman married to a nonbeliever and you are under stress because your husband doesn't care anything about the Lord or the Bible or doing the right things. So you come to me as your pastor and say, "I'm really unhappy being married to this nonbeliever, and a few weeks ago, I met a really nice man at church who loves the Lord. And would you believe it, Greg? The Lord actually spoke to me and said I should dump my non-Christian husband and marry this good, kind Christian man."

But God *didn't* say that, and He *wouldn't* say that. His Word says, "If a Christian woman has a husband who is not a believer and he is willing to continue living with her, she must not leave him" (verse 13, NLT). In fact, it's this Christian woman's job to try to win her husband to Christ.

But what if the nonbeliever walks out on the marriage and abandons you, the believing partner? According to Scripture, if that happens, you are free. You don't have to remain in that relationship, and you are free ultimately to remarry.

These biblical exceptions for divorce, however, don't happen very often. Most marriages fail because of selfishness and because the husband and wife ignore what the Bible says and do what they want to do.

C. S. Lewis put it this way:

> People get from books the idea that if you have married the right person you may expect to go on "being in love" forever. As a result, when they find they are not, they think this proves they made a mistake and are entitled to a change — not realizing that, when they have changed, the glamour will presently go out of the new love just as it went out of the old one.
>
> In this department of life, as in every other, thrills come at the beginning and do not last. . . . If you go through with it, the dying away of the first thrill will be compensated for by a quieter and more lasting kind of interest.[2]

Does Cathe still thrill me? You bet she does. But it's not like I swoon or get light-headed every time I pass her in the hallway at home or see her in the kitchen cooking breakfast. The love we have for each other now is far deeper and more significant than that original attraction, when we both had stars in our eyes. Sometimes we feel it, and at other times we don't. Nevertheless, it's always there, a constant in our lives and an unbelievable comfort in times of trials and sorrow.

We've all heard of the fairy-tale romances in which the

prince and princess live "happily ever after." I think a better way to say it would be, "They lived happily *even* after."

After what? After marriage.

Because they did it God's way.

CHAPTER FIVE

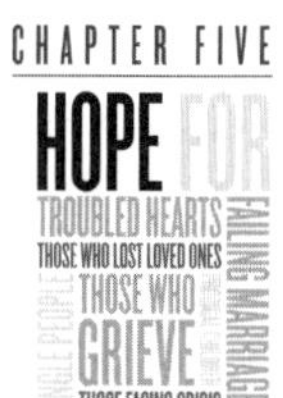

HOPE FOR HURTING MARRIAGES

PART 2

JOHN AND CHRISTY MET in their high school history class and became good friends. As time went on, they began dating and then went steady. Eventually, after they graduated from high school, John proposed, Christy accepted, and the wedding day finally came. John could hardly believe his good fortune as his beautiful bride made her way down that aisle.

They stood in front of the pastor in the church and repeated those sacred vows. It was almost surreal to her. She kept asking herself, *Is this really happening?*

They were officially pronounced husband and wife, and off they went on their honeymoon. They didn't have a lot of money, but they were able to rent a little apartment and set up housekeeping. Their first three pieces of furniture came from IKEA. They didn't have the money for going out or for a lot of fancy meals, but they were together. They studied the Bible together, prayed together, and tried to plug into a young-marrieds group at church. They were inseparable. You couldn't even say "John" without saying "Christy." They were like one person.

Fast-forward ten years. John has worked very hard, and his career has taken off. Now they have a very nice home. In fact, Christy is also working, part-time, to help make the house payment. They have two children, a boy and a girl.

The problem is, they're both so busy that they don't see much of each other anymore. It's not because they *have* to spend so much time apart; it's because they have chosen to, because far too often their conversations turn into arguments, usually about money.

Christy goes to the gym four days a week and is in the best shape of her life. John, however, couldn't fit back into that wedding tuxedo if his life depended upon it. Besides that, John has just hired a cute new executive assistant that he's spending a lot of time with. And Christy? She has found herself attracted to her trainer down at the gym.

What is happening here?

The inevitable split is beginning to take place.

John and Christy are spending more and more time apart. It's like they hardly know each other anymore. Finally Christy says, "I'm leaving you." Deep down, she hopes John will stop her, but he doesn't.

And weeks turn into months.

Now a year has passed, and they decide to get a divorce and retain lawyers. Nevertheless, they make a promise to each other. This will be a "civil" divorce. They had been friends for so long, so why should they be enemies?

So it starts out being cool, calm, and civil. But it doesn't stay civil for very long. All too soon, civility gives way to anger, anger to resentment, resentment to bitterness, and their best friend has now become their worst enemy.

You have heard this story before. It's not a true story, but it's a composite drawn from many stories I have heard over the years of how marriages start to unravel. It happens far too often. To quote Freddie Mercury, "Another one bites the dust."

Some might say, "That's just the way it goes in the real world. People can't stay together forever, especially if the love is gone. It's sort of like trading your car in for the new model. That's just the way it happens."

I suggest to you that this is *not* the way it has to happen.

I believe that you can have love that will last you for a lifetime. I can speak to this with some authority because my wife, Cathe, and I have been married for thirty-eight years.

"Well," someone will reply, "you guys are just anomalies. You're not like real people living in the real world. You probably didn't even have to make any adjustments."

Let me tell you this: Greg and Cathe are about as opposite from each other as you can get. It used to surprise me that we see everything so differently, but I stopped being surprised a long time ago.

I told you in the previous chapter that Cathe is very neat and I'm fairly messy. But get this: She likes weird food, such as Indian cuisine and Thai food, and I like hamburgers and burritos. I am always in a rush, and she is the definition of laid-back.

We are very different.

That is the way it goes when you put two people together for a lifetime. You're going to have differences. But wasn't it those very differences that initially attracted you to one another? Didn't you used to laugh about those things? But now somehow those differences have become "irreconcilable." (Terrible word!) What I am saying to you is that you can get through *any* rough patch that you may be experiencing in your marriage today.

The fact is, you can get through a difficult season in your marriage if you just press on and don't give up. If you can hold your course and get some help, things truly can improve. Through my years in the ministry, I have witnessed the most incredible marriage turnaround stories you could imagine. Believe me, wherever you are in your marriage, there is hope.

The thoughts I'd like to share with you in this chapter are neither new nor revolutionary. But they have one thing going for them: They actually work.

Here's what it comes down to: Do you want a marriage that will last a lifetime? Do you truly *want* it? How much do you want it? Are you willing to apply yourself in order to achieve it?

You can turn your marriage into a classic.

Some years ago, I owned a 1957 Bel Air convertible. That was a killer car. I got an amazing deal on it, and it was in perfect condition, with everything original. The problem with my '57 Chevy was the color. It was called Tropical Turquoise. I liked it, but no one else did. So I would drive it around, but my wife didn't want to ride with me. She would say, "I feel like we're in a parade or something. I don't want to ride in that car."

I would pick up my son from surfing, and it would embarrass him when I would pull up in my amazingly turquoise '57. He would say, "Dad, could you not pick me up in that car?" The only one who would drive with me in the car was the dog. So I did a lot of cruising around with the dog, which wasn't quite what I was hoping for.

Wherever I would go, however, people would inevitably come up to me and ask, "What year is it?" I would be telling people over and over again, "1957 . . . 1957 . . . 1957." People kept asking because it was amazing to see such a gorgeous classic on the road, looking like it was brand-new. You just don't see many classics like that anymore.

The same can be true of your marriage. In this day and age, with so many divorces and failing marriages all around, if you have been married for thirty, forty, or fifty years, that's pretty unusual. Someone will ask Cathe and me how long we have been married, and we will say, "Thirty-eight years."

And they will say, "What? Was she nine years old when you married her?"

The point is, your marriage can turn into a classic too—a real beauty that will turn heads, turn hearts, and last for the rest of your lives.

But let me offer this caution: Our contemporary culture never will be the friend of your marriage. In fact, the world we live in today is actively hostile toward marriage and the family and will try to erode or undermine those vital relationships at every turn.

The only source of help, the only wellspring of wisdom that offers any help and hope for marriages and the family today, is the powerful, changeless Word of God.

What does God's Word say? That is a question that will lead you to the right answers every time.

STRONG HELP FOR EVERY MARRIAGE

I have never met a husband and wife who were considering a divorce who were actually doing what we're about to read together in Ephesians 5.

Let me repeat that: In forty years of pastoral ministry, I have never met a husband and wife who were following the directions of Ephesians 5 and still considering a divorce. On the other hand, I have met quite a number of couples who were not willing to follow the apostle Paul's counsel and ended up in bitter divorces.

Reading these words alone, of course, won't save any marriage. You must act on them. You must *do* them. And they are doable by the power of the Holy Spirit. These words are current. They don't need to be updated or refreshed. They don't need to be rewritten to align with what is politically correct. They simply need to be implemented to be effective.

Paul begins with a word directed at husbands.

"Husbands, Love Your Wives"

> Husbands, love your wives, just as Christ also loved the church and gave Himself for her, that He might sanctify and cleanse her with the washing of water by the word, that He might present her to Himself a glorious church, not having spot or wrinkle or any such thing, but that she should be holy and without blemish. So husbands ought to love their own wives as their own bodies; he who loves his wife loves himself. For no one ever hated his own flesh, but nourishes and cherishes it, just as the Lord does the church. For we are members of His body, of His flesh and of His bones. "For this reason a man shall leave his father and mother and be joined to his wife, and the two

> shall become one flesh." This is a great mystery, but I speak concerning Christ and the church. Nevertheless let each one of you in particular so love his own wife as himself, and let the wife see that she respects her husband. (Ephesians 5:25-33)

Four times in eight verses, husbands are told to love their wives. And how are we to love our wives? Paul says we are to love them "as Christ also loved the church" (verse 25). A tall order, you say? Yes, it is. But if men would start doing that one thing, it would transform their marriages.

I heard a story of a couple who went to see a pastor. They were on the verge of a divorce, and they basically wanted the pastor to agree that divorce was an acceptable resolution to their problems. They sat down with him, and he listened for a while as they related their sad, all-too-common story.

Suddenly the pastor turned to the husband and said, "The Bible says you are to love your wife as Christ loved the church."

"Oh," the husband replied, "I could never do that. That's setting the bar too high. I could never live up to that."

The pastor said, "All right. If you can't do that, let's lower it a level. The Bible says you are supposed to love your neighbor as yourself."

Again the husband said, "I couldn't do that, either."

"All right," the pastor replied. "The Bible also says to love your enemies. *Begin there!*"

There's no getting off the hook on this. If you are a husband, you are to love your wife. The Greek term Paul used here is *agape*, a word for love the New Testament uses more than any other.

This is the same word used in 1 Corinthians 13, where it is broken out and defined. It's the word used in John 3:16, where it says, "For God so loved [*agaped*] the world." It is the word used to describe God Himself, when the Bible says that "God is love." This is a supernatural love that can be experienced only by the Christian. The Bible says that this *agape*-love is poured out in our hearts by the Holy Spirit (see Romans 5:5). It is the fruit of the Spirit (see Galatians 5:22).

If you are a Christian in a living relationship with Jesus Christ, you should be showing forth this love in your life. The nonbeliever, on the other hand, has no access to this supernatural love.

Why is this important? Because the Christian has the clear advantage in the marriage. So don't tell me that you, as two Christians, can't work out your differences in a marriage! Don't tell me that you have "irreconcilable differences." (Do you get the idea that I hate this term?) Are you telling me that Christ is not living in you and your spouse? Are you telling me that God could not intervene and help you? Are you telling me that your situation is hopeless?

God, in His wisdom, has picked one symbol to visibly show to a lost world His love for the church and the church's love for Him, and it is the Christian marriage. He says, in effect, "World, check this out. Do you see the way that husband loves his wife? Do you see the way he is laying down his life for her? *That* is how I love the church. And do you see the way that wife respects her husband and submits to his leadership? That is the way My church submits to Me."

Irreconcilable differences? In a *Christian* couple? Are you kidding me? What a horrible testimony that is! And tell me this: How could such a thing even develop if the husband in that marriage set out, with all his strength and the help of God Himself, to love his wife? And guess what? It doesn't matter if she doesn't happen to be "lovable" at the time. That doesn't change our privilege and responsibility one iota.

In his excellent book *Love Life for Every Married Couple*, Dr. Ed Wheat wrote,

> Even in the best of marriages unlovable traits show up in both partners. And in every marriage, sooner or later, a need arises that can be met only by unconditional love. *Agape* is the answer for all the woundings of marriage. This love has the capacity to persist in the face of rejection and continue on when there is no response at all. It can leap over walls that would stop any human love cold. It is never deflected by unlovable behavior and gives gladly to the undeserving without totalling the cost. . . . *Agape* is the Divine solution for marriages populated by imperfect human beings![1]

We need God's eternal love.

Before continuing on in Ephesians 5, let's briefly check out the Bible's description of *agape* love in 1 Corinthians 13. In this passage, Paul didn't define love as much as he showed us what love does. And every time you read the word *love* here, it is the word *agape*.

> Love suffers long and is kind; love does not envy; love does not parade itself, is not puffed up; does not behave rudely, does not seek its own, is not provoked, thinks no evil; does not rejoice in iniquity, but rejoices in the truth; bears all things, believes all things, hopes all things, endures all things. Love never fails. (verses 4-8)

A more modern translation of the same passage reads like this:

> Love never gives up.
> Love cares more for others than for self.
> Love doesn't want what it doesn't have.
> Love doesn't strut,
> Doesn't have a swelled head,
> Doesn't force itself on others,
> Isn't always "me first,"
> Doesn't fly off the handle,
> Doesn't keep score of the sins of others,
> Doesn't revel when others grovel,
> Takes pleasure in the flowering of truth,
> Puts up with anything,
> Trusts God always,
> Always looks for the best,
> Never looks back,
> But keeps going to the end.
> Love never dies. (MSG)

Husbands, are you loving your wife that way? That is the kind of love Scripture tells us we should have.

Yes, we would all admit to falling short. I would be the first to admit that I don't always love my wife that way. If you want to feel really bad, take out the word *love* in 1 Corinthians and insert your own name in its place. *GREG suffers long and is kind. GREG never envies. GREG is never rude. GREG is never provoked.* It doesn't always work out that way, does it?

But I will tell you a name that does work very well. Put

"Jesus" in there in place of the word *love* and it fits perfectly. First Corinthians 13 is a portrait of Jesus.

These aren't just nice, poetic-sounding words; this is real life. This is what we actually should aspire to. It is not something abstract or passive; it is active and functioning. Love doesn't just feel patient; it *practices* patience. It doesn't just have kind feelings; it *does* kind things.

Love is only love when it acts. The apostle John wrote, "Let us not love in word or in tongue, but in deed and in truth" (1 John 3:18). Another translation says, "Let us stop just *saying* we love people; let us *really* love them, and *show it* by our *actions*" (TLB).

So please don't say to me, "We've tried everything," because you haven't tried this. If you were trying this, your marriage wouldn't be in trouble. So many times, couples in trouble end up in marriage counseling. And that can be a wise course of action if you're sure the counselor will give you true biblical counsel and not just a bunch of human theories.

Before you pick up the phone to call a counselor, Christian husband, just try doing it the way God tells you to do it. Try it for a week. Do everything you can possibly do to love your wife with the *agape* supernatural love of Jesus Christ for a week and see what a difference that will make.

I heard a story of a drunk man who was searching under a streetlight for his wallet. Someone asked him, "Did you lose your wallet near here?"

"No," he replied, "I lost it two blocks over that way."

"Well, then, why aren't you looking over there?"

"Because there's no streetlight."

It doesn't do any good to look for something if you're

looking in the wrong place. The right place is the Word of God. The wrong place is the advice of friends, family, or non-biblical counselors.

WHAT IS GOD TELLING HUSBANDS?

1. If you really love your wife, you will be patient with her.

> "Love is patient." (1 Corinthians 13:4, NIV)

Literally, the word here is *long-tempered.* It's a common term in the New Testament and is used almost exclusively to mean being patient with people rather than circumstances or events. Be patient with her; have a long fuse before you get irritated or cross or angry or cutting or sarcastic.

"Well, Greg, she isn't being a very good wife to me right now."

It doesn't matter! Cut her lots of slack and wait for God's timing. The more of God's love you demonstrate to her, the more (in time) she will respond with love in return.

2. If you really love your wife, you will show kindness and tenderness to her.

> "Love is kind." (verse 4, NIV)

Just as patience will take anything from others, kindness will give anything to others. If a husband loves his wife like this, she will respond appropriately. Think of it like this: Why do we love God today? Because He won us over with His love and amazing kindness. The Bible says, "We love Him because

He first loved us" (1 John 4:19). Our love is a response to His love. The Scripture goes on to say, "God's kindness leads you toward repentance" (Romans 2:4, NIV).

I will often talk to husbands who complain about their wives who "aren't doing their part." Oh, really? Why don't you do *your* part? As the husband, you are charged by God to be the spiritual leader and the initiator in your marriage. So what am I suggesting here? I'm suggesting that if you do your part, in most cases she will do her part. Are there exceptions to this? Of course, but that's what they are: exceptions.

Husband, are you kind to your wife? Sometimes we show more kindness to a complete stranger than we do to the one who is flesh of our flesh and bone of our bone. Here is a way to show your kindness: Just tell her how much you appreciate her. When is the last time you told your wife how much you loved her or how beautiful she was?

"Well, Greg, sometimes I think those things but don't say them."

So say it. Verbalize a little. No, we may not be as verbal as women. But if we're interested in something—a certain sports team or a car or a project—we can speak well enough. So give it a shot! Start saying kind things to your wife, not to get something back from her but just to be kind, as God has been to you.

Studies have revealed that women speak an average of 50,000 words a day, while men speak half that many. As simple as it sounds, I would suggest that a hug and a kiss would go a long way.

Some German researchers put a great deal of money into a project aimed toward finding the secret to a long life and success. Do you know what they discovered? The secret was in a kiss. They said that if you kiss your wife every morning when you leave for work, you will live longer and be more successful in life. They said that the good-morning kissers missed less work because of sickness and earned 20 to 30 percent more money than the non-kissers. Now, there is something to think about.

3. If you really love your wife, you will do it and not just talk about it.

> "Love . . . does not boast." (I Corinthians 13:4, NIV)

In other words, it doesn't parade itself or talk about itself. Love doesn't say, "Do you know how much I do for you? Do you know how hard I work for you? Do you know the sacrifice? Do you remember the stuff I did for you on Saturday?"

Yeah, yeah, yeah. She probably knows that stuff. So why spoil it all by bringing it up and boasting about it? Just do acts of love; don't speak of them.

4. If you really love your wife, you will treat her with respect.

> "Love . . . is not rude." (verses 4-5, NIV)

Love does not behave rudely, period. Don't be short with your wife. Don't be harsh with your wife. Don't tear her down or demean her, not in private and certainly not in front of others. When you are in public with your wife, you should take every opportunity to compliment her and build her up. In Proverbs 31, after we read a description of the virtuous woman, we read in verse 28 that "her husband . . . praises her."

I love to hear that. I love it when a husband builds up his wife in front of friends. It's especially nice when a dad praises the mom in the family in front of the children. "Let me tell you about your mother, kids. Your mom is the best. She is one in a million."

What if you don't feel it? Do it anyway.

If you have a critical word for your wife, save it for when you're alone and at home. Or better still, chuck it in the trash can and forget about it. Don't argue or correct your wife in front of others, even if she corrects you. You're a man, with broad shoulders, so just take it. And be especially careful about speaking of her in a negative way in front of the children or—worse still—asking your kids to take sides. That is a horrible thing to do to your sons and daughters as well as your wife.

5. If you really love your wife, you will not be harsh with her.

> "Love . . . is not easily angered." (1 Corinthians 13:4-5, NIV)

There will be times when you disagree with your wife. But if those disagreements turn into shouting matches, you have gone too far. Shouting in anger or irritation is never productive. Ephesians 4:26-27 adds this bit of helpful counsel: "Do not let the sun go down on your wrath, nor give place to the devil." In other words, don't ever go to bed angry at each other.

I heard about a husband and wife who decided to put this principle into practice. After thirty years of marriage, they had never violated this. They had never gone to bed mad at each other.

Someone asked the husband, "How did that work out?"

He replied, "It was all right, I guess, but it was hard sitting up all night sometimes!"

6. If you really love your wife, you will always believe the best, not the worst, about her.

> "Love . . . keeps no record of wrongs." (1 Corinthians 13:4-5, NIV)

The Scripture uses a bookkeeping term here that means "to calculate" or "enter into a ledger." This is when you're having an argument and reach back into time for some old offense that should have been forgotten: "Well, I remember twenty years ago, when you said . . ."

What? Twenty years ago? Get rid of those old memories and past hurts. "Forgive as the Lord forgave you" (Colossians 3:13, NIV). Would you want the Lord digging up your old sins and throwing them in front of your face again? Of course not. He has buried them in the deepest sea.

So how about the other side of the picture?

WHAT DOES EPHESIANS 5 HAVE TO SAY TO WIVES?

> Wives, submit to your own husbands, as to the Lord. For the husband is head of the wife, as also Christ is head of the church; and He is the Savior of the body. Therefore, just as the church is subject to Christ, so let the wives be to their own husbands in everything. (Ephesians 5:22-24)

You may remember that in the previous chapter, we touched on Ephesians 5:21: "submitting to one another in the fear of God."

People choke on the word *submit.* Men choke on it, and women choke on it. But we all submit, in one way or another. We submit to the laws of the land when we get behind the wheel of our car (or at least, we had better). We submit to the police officer when he tells us to pull over to the side of the road. We submit to the government when the tax bill comes in. We submit to our employer if we want to keep our job. We submit to a teacher or professor who gives us an assignment to turn in.

We all submit in life.

We are all under authority.

That is just the way society works. It's the way that *life* works.

As we noted in the last chapter, *submit* is a military term that means "to rank under." But notice once again that before Scripture says anything about wives submitting to husbands, it says that we need to submit "to one another in the fear of God." This implies a true partnership, and it means that you have your mate's interests in mind. You want to do whatever you can to lift him up. You want to build her up. You are his number one fan. She is yours. He knows you are always in his corner and vice versa. *That* is the idea of submitting. We are holding one another up and building one another up.

A loving wife will submit to the servant leadership of her husband. And if he is doing all of those things we have mentioned in this chapter—loving her, valuing her, honoring her, and being kind and patient with her—it will make her task that much easier.

My suggestion to both husbands and wives is to stop reading each other's mail. By that I mean that husbands should stop quoting this verse about the wife submitting and wives should stop quoting the verses about the husband's responsibility in the marriage.

Husband, why don't you just focus on your part and do what God asks you to do? And, wives, why don't you do the same with the verses God has directed toward you?

Just do your part, and watch what happens.

Yes, it does say that a wife needs to submit to the leadership of her husband. This is not implying that the man is better than the woman or that the woman is better than the man. (They're just very, very different!) The fact of the matter is that when it comes to our relationship with God, we have equal access. Galatians 3:28 tells us that in Christ "there is neither Jew nor Greek, there is neither slave nor free, there is neither male nor female."

If you as a wife struggle with this idea of the husband being the spiritual leader or head of the home, consider the words of Paul in 1 Corinthians 11:3: "I want you to know that the head of every man is Christ, the head of woman is man, and the head of Christ is God."

The head of Christ is God? Is God the Father "better" than God the Son? Of course not. They are coequal and coeternal. The Bible is saying that God the Father is the head of Christ, not in essence or in nature but in function. When Jesus came to this earth, even though He was God, He humbled Himself and laid aside His privileges. He took upon Himself the form of a servant and submitted to the will of the Father. In the Garden of Gethsemane, He prayed, "Nevertheless, not My will but Yours be done" (Luke 22:42).

Jesus submitted to that authority, because there is a structure within the nature of the Godhead. Paul refers to that structure and applies it to the marriage relationship.

The biblical structure for a marriage, then, is that the husband is the spiritual leader, and the wife submits to that leadership.

Then what about the man who doesn't seek his wife's input on the decisions of life? He's an idiot. A husband and wife are *partners*. I frankly can't think of a time in thirty-eight years of marriage where I have said to Cathe, "We're going to do this because I am head of the home."

No, Cathe and I always talk about our choices and decisions. I would be a fool not to do that. Why? Because I value her input. I value her wisdom, and I honor her perspective as a woman, wife, and mother. We usually come to a decision *together*. In Proverbs 31, we read that the husband has "full confidence" in his wife (verse 11, NIV). "She speaks with wisdom, and faithful instruction is on her tongue" (verse 26, NIV).

A wise man will listen to his wise wife.

What is the motive of submission? Ephesians 5:22 tells wives to submit to their husbands "as to the Lord." There may be times when you don't want to submit to your husband's authority, but you do it "as to the Lord." In that moment, you are submitting to Christ.

This is true for everyone, however. If you have a job and have difficulty submitting to your supervisor, you do it as unto the Lord. Colossians 3:23 says, "Work willingly at whatever you do, as though you were working for the Lord rather than for people" (NLT).

In other words, you aren't working just for the paycheck or to please the boss, but you are working as unto Jesus. You're doing it for Him, to please Him.

Are there limits to submission? Does a wife do whatever her husband asks, no matter what? Yes, there are certainly limits. If your husband would ever ask you to do something that is unbiblical, you are not required to submit. Let's say you have a non-Christian husband who says, "I no longer want you to go to church or read the Bible or pray, and you must stop because I am head of the home."

Do you say, "Okay, honey, I will just submit"?

No. You say, "I love you as my husband, but I will continue to go to church, read my Bible, and pray."

As the apostles said, "We must obey God rather than any human authority" (Acts 5:29, NLT).

THERE IS HOPE

There is hope today for your failing marriage. You need to humble yourself before God, come to Him, and ask Him to help you.

Having said that, however, don't just sit around waiting for a miracle. He has already given you everything you need to cope with life (see 2 Peter 1:3). He has given you the power, resources, direction, and wisdom in His Word.

The question is, what will you do with those supernatural resources? Nothing really happens until you begin doing what He has called you to do. Don't wait for some surge of emotional love to come over you. Just start doing the right things. Start loving. Start helping in practical ways. Start showing kindness. Even if you don't feel like it, just roll up your sleeves and start doing it, trusting the Lord for His strength. And then watch how God can begin to change your marriage.

In the book of Revelation, there is a message to the Ephesians who were drifting away from their love commitment to Christ. As a result, Jesus gave them this prescription for restoration. He said in Revelation 2:5, "Remember the height from which you have fallen! Repent and do the things you did at first" (NIV).

The way to get right with God, then, is to remember, repent, and repeat.

We could apply that principle to a marriage, too.

First, remember. It used to be better than it is now. You used to go out together and do this and that and had such a happy time together. So when is the last time you did any of those things you used to do? Take your wife out to dinner. Write her little notes. Bring her flowers now and then. Go to the park for a picnic. Get back to doing what you used to do when you were so much closer and were having such a great life together.

Your marriage is bigger than you and your spouse and your children, if you have any. God deliberately brought you together to give this poor, mixed-up culture a picture of the love of Jesus Christ for His people, His church. Don't ruin that picture by neglecting your marriage and letting it fall apart.

God can heal your hurting marriage, beginning today, if you will let Him.

HOPE FOR THOSE WITH PRODIGAL CHILDREN

HAVE YOU EVER LOST anything?

Of course you have. And the older you get, the more things you lose. I have walked around the house looking for my reading glasses, only to walk by a mirror and see them perched on top of my head.

When I was a little boy, I had a parakeet named Popcorn. He was a fantastic little bird! I would stand a few feet away from his cage, open the little door and call his name, and he would fly and land on my shoulder. And then I would walk around the house with him on my shoulder.

One day I was down on Balboa Island in Newport Beach and saw a guy walking around with a parrot on his shoulder. It amazed me that the bird just stayed there and didn't fly away. My little brain processed this, and I thought, *I could do that with Popcorn.*

So I went home, got Popcorn, and put him on my shoulder. Then I walked outside, and Popcorn flew away! I never saw him again. For days after, I literally walked down the street calling, "Popcorn! Popcorn!" (People who saw me probably thought, *The poor kid is starving. Somebody ought to give him some food.*)

Fast-forward with me now a number of years. I'm married, and Christopher is just a little boy. We had just obtained a puppy that we named Biscuit, but he got loose in the neighborhood somewhere, and we couldn't find him.

So guess who went up and down the street calling, "Biscuit! Biscuit!"?

(And people looking out their windows were probably wondering, *Does this man need some food?*)

Fortunately we found Biscuit, and we were all happy about that.

It's one thing to lose a parakeet or a puppy, but it's something else entirely to lose a child.

In one of our out-of-town crusades years ago, our family was staying in a hotel. Jonathan was about five years old at the time. I was walking with him when he spied the elevator and ran ahead of me because he loved to push the buttons. "Wait for me!" I called to him. "Don't get in the elevator until Dad gets there."

But just as I came around the corner, I saw Jonathan standing in the elevator, and the doors slid shut. I thought I would have a heart attack on the spot! I pushed every button I could see and waited for the elevator to come back.

Have you ever noticed that constantly pushing the button on an elevator doesn't get it to you any faster? Finally the elevator arrived, but when the door opened, there was no Jonathan.

I took the elevator down to the lobby and ran up to the front desk, where the employee was on the phone. "Excuse me, ma'am," I said. "My little son just got off the elevator—somewhere? Can you call security?" I wanted security, the police, a SWAT team, the Navy SEALs—whoever could help me find our little boy.

But she wouldn't even get off the phone! In fact, she turned her back on me.

I kept saying, "Ma'am, excuse me, excuse me . . ." but I was being ignored. I thought, *Okay, I've got to find him myself.* So I went back to the elevator and pushed every button for every floor, and each time the door opened up, I yelled his name as loud as I could.

I would have torn that hotel apart, room by room, to find him. Losing him was not an option. Well, I did find him. I don't know what floor it was on, but he was just standing there and I swept him up into my arms.

So it is one thing to lose a pet. But losing a son or daughter is infinitely worse than that.

As Christian parents, our greatest joy is in seeing our kids walk with the Lord. As the apostle John said, "I have no greater joy than to hear that my children walk in truth" (3 John 4). As believers, then, we seek to raise our kids in the way of the Lord, and we do all we can to show them the right way to live.

But sometimes they go astray anyway.

When children are very young, they're more open, receptive, compliant, and obedient. In fact, for a time, a son or daughter will think that you hung the moon and that whatever Mom or Dad says must obviously be true.

As they get older, however, especially when they enter their teenage years, they start to push back. They start to think for themselves, and sometimes they begin to question the faith with which they have been raised.

Mark Twain once said, "When I was a boy of fourteen, my father was so ignorant I could hardly stand to have the old man around. But when I got to be twenty-one, I was astonished by how much he'd learned in seven years."

This is the way the teenage brain works. Teens think they are older than they really are and know more than they really know. They look at you, the parent, and question many of the things you have said to them.

ON LOAN FROM GOD

I cannot emphasize enough how important it is to have a godly home and what a significant role you play as a Christian dad or mom in a child's life. The psalmist wrote,

> Children are a gift from the Lord;
> they are a reward from him.
> Children born to a young man
> are like arrows in a warrior's hands.
> How joyful is the man whose quiver is full of them! (Psalm 127:3-5, NLT)

Children are gifts. We don't own them; they belong to God. They're not ours to mold but rather to unfold—to nurture and raise in the way of the Lord.

Sometimes you will hear parents say, "We never really

had any problems with our kids. They have never rebelled."

"Really? How old are your children?"

"Four and five."

Come to me after you've raised teenagers and lived to tell the story. Maybe then I'll listen to you.

Again, to quote Mark Twain, "Things run along pretty smoothly until your kid reaches thirteen. That's the time you need to stick 'em in a barrel, hammer the lid down nice and snug, and feed 'em through the knothole. And then, about the time he turns sixteen, plug up the knothole!"

We live in a culture that is hostile to the family—a culture that, for the most part, influences our children in wrong directions. At best, it ignores the values we have raised them with. At worst, it seeks to undermine or mock those values. As a result, we want to make sure we are doing our part to counteract those negative, degrading influences and give our kids a good foundation on which to build their future lives.

A "DON'T" AND A "DO"

Ephesians 6:4 says, "Fathers, do not provoke your children to wrath, but bring them up in the training and admonition of the Lord." This verse of Scripture tells us both what *not* to do and what *to* do. On the negative side, the verse tells us not to provoke our children or anger them. The original language suggests a repeated pattern of treatment that causes a child to have anger and resentment that boils over to outright hostility.

So how would we do that? One way is by showing

favoritism. This often happens in a family. A parent will favor one child over another. Kids figure this out really quickly, by the way, and this can develop both unhealthy rivalry and deep resentment among the children.

In the Bible, we remember the story of Isaac and Rebekah and their two sons, Esau and Jacob. Clearly, Isaac favored Esau, while Rebekah favored Jacob. This fueled a rivalry between those brothers that lasted a lifetime. At one point, Esau became so bitter toward his fraternal twin that he plotted to murder him. What's the bottom line here? Just try to be evenhanded in the way you treat your children.

Another way to "provoke your children to wrath" is by withholding affirming words, encouragement, or compliments from them. A child craves and *needs* approval and encouragement for things they do well as much as they need correction when they misbehave. We're usually quick to tell our kids when they're wrong or where they're falling short. But do we notice the positive things they do and affirm them for it?

"Good job!"

"Wow, did you color that? It's beautiful!"

"You look so nice this morning."

"You have a real talent for that."

Of course, this also can be overdone. In our contemporary culture, some people overpraise their sons and daughters. It has been described by some experts as "helicopter parenting." The idea is that the parent is always hovering over the child, praising everything he or she does. You can overcorrect your children and never affirm, but you can also overaffirm, giving them credit for something they really shouldn't get credit for.

"Way to finish your meal. You are the best."

No, they just finished their meal. It's not an occasion for praise.

I was surprised to learn that in competitive sports among children today, the adults don't even keep score. In some classrooms, they don't give out grades. Why? Because they don't want to make one child feel like he or she is less than another child. In those instances, the pendulum has swung too far the other way.

To withhold appropriate affirmation, however, can be one of those ways that we "provoke [our] children to wrath." Instead, the verse tells us, we are to "bring them up in the training and instruction of the Lord" (NIV). It doesn't say beat them down; it says bring them up. That phrase, *bring them up*, means to nourish or feed. So we want to encourage our children as they grow and change. We want to teach them good manners and to be hardworking and responsible. But the most important thing we do with our kids or for our kids is point them to Jesus Christ.

But here is something to remember: We cannot lead a child any further in a walk with God than we ourselves have come. Nothing can happen *through* us until it has happened *to* us. This means that we as parents need to cultivate an authentic, passionate, disciplined walk with the living God. As Paul wrote in Philippians 4:9, "Whatever you have learned or received or heard from me, or seen in me—put it into practice. And the God of peace will be with you" (NIV).

I read the story of a father and son who were climbing a mountain. They came to a place where the climbing was difficult and even dangerous, and the father stopped to consider which way to go. Behind him, his little boy said, "Choose the right path, Dad. I'm coming right behind you." And that is something to remember as parents. Your children are watching you, so choose the right path. In the long run, they won't just do what you say; they will do what you do.

So how do we accomplish this? How do we raise our children in the way of the Lord? We do it by spending a lot of time with them. People talk today about "quality time versus quantity time." Don't let that become an excuse to cut back on the time you spend with your sons and daughters. Kids need lots and lots of time. Spend as much time with them as you possibly can. And then, through those minutes and hours you spend together, use every opportunity to teach them the things of God. Yes, it's good to talk about the Bible and Jesus in bedtime stories or in a short devotional you might have with your kids, but it's even more effective to talk about the Lord and find opportune teaching moments throughout the course of a day together.

In Deuteronomy 6:7, we read that Israelite parents were to diligently teach God's words to their children. The passage goes on to say, "You shall . . . talk of them when you sit in your house, when you walk by the way, when you lie down, and when you rise up."

In other words, you talk about God all day long.

You watch for teaching opportunities all day long.

Some Christian parents attempt to protect their kids from our corrupt contemporary culture by locking things down—doing their best not to allow any secular input in their home at all. But even if you don't have TV, your kids will still see TV at their friends' houses, at the mall, or somewhere else. Even if you don't have the Internet, your kids will still access the Internet on their cell phone or on their friend's cell phone. One way or another, the culture will influence your children. You can't weave them inside a tight Christian cocoon and expect them to stay there always.

I don't think *isolating* children from the culture is nearly as effective as *preparing* children for those cultural issues with a Christian worldview.

When our son Christopher was very young and wanted to watch various cartoons on TV, I would sometimes sit down and watch with him. I would laugh at the things that were funny, and if anything was subversive or contrary to our faith, I would point it out to him. I was trying to help him learn how to think for himself.

I read an interview by a contemporary performer who was raised in a Christian home and used to sing Christian music. In the article, she said that her parents had banned all secular music in their home. In fact, they went to such lengths that they wouldn't use the terms *deviled eggs* or *Dirt Devil vacuum* because they didn't want anyone to even speak the word *devil.* The young woman said that her friends would sneak secular music into her room and she would listen to it. She went on to say that because her parents were so stern, she "had no childhood" and eventually rebelled.

Today she seems miles from the Lord. I pray for her that she will come back to the Lord. And I would eat a deviled egg with her anytime.

"TRAIN UP A CHILD"

One of the frequently quoted—and frequently misunderstood—verses about raising children is Proverbs 22:6:

"Train up a child in the way he should go, and when he is old he will not depart from it." We usually will quote this verse when one of our kids has turned away from the Lord and gone his or her own way. We quote it in the hope that our prodigal one day will turn back to the Lord again.

I don't refute that; it's a good verse to quote. But let's just hope that we actually did what the Scripture says.

What does it mean when it says, "Train up a child in the way he should go"? It's an interesting phrase in the original language. It speaks of the actions of a midwife, who, after delivering a child, would put her finger into crushed dates and place it in the baby's mouth, thereby creating a thirst for milk. Playing out that idea, we might conclude that Scripture is urging us to create a thirst in our children for spiritual things.

That same word, however, could be used to speak of a horse being brought into submission to its rider as a cowboy would break a wild horse for the saddle. When you put that all together, you have the idea that as Christian parents, we ought to provide parameters as well as motivation for our children to walk with the Lord.

But what does it mean when it says "a child"? When does child raising stop? In several instances in the Old Testament, this word is translated as "infant." In another place, it speaks of a young boy. It is also used to describe Ishmael in his preteen years and Joseph, son of Jacob, at age seventeen. In yet another verse, it is used to speak of a young man ready for marriage. "Child," therefore, speaks of infancy to young adulthood. So don't imagine that your child-raising days are over once your kids hit the teen years. It goes on—both the responsibility and the opportunity to set a wise and godly example for your sons and daughters.

To put it all together, here is what I believe Proverbs 22:6 is saying to us: Create a spiritual thirst and appetite in your child from his or her earliest days. And from infancy into young adulthood, build into your son or daughter the experience of submission. As parents, we are to provide both external boundaries as well as internal motivation.

The verse says, "Train a child *in the way he should go.*" Every child has his or her own bent. Even children born to the same parents and in the same family can be very different. I think of my own two sons, Christopher and Jonathan. With Christopher, I would tell him something and then have to tell him again three minutes later! I would tell him again and again and again, and he would still disobey me. With Jonathan, I would tell him once, and that would do it. In fact, I really wouldn't need to say anything to Jonathan; if I just looked at him with disapproval, he would melt.

Each child has his or her own personality, or bent. And Scripture is telling us to recognize those differences and adjust our parenting accordingly.

THE SON WHO LEFT BUT ALSO RETURNED

Perhaps you would say, "Greg, we've trained our child in the way of the Lord to the best of our ability. We've done everything we know to do, but our child went astray anyway. We must be failures as parents."

Not so fast! If having a prodigal son or daughter means you are a failure as a parent, that means God must be a failure because He has many prodigals. Obviously, God is not a failure as a Father, and having a rebellious child doesn't mean you are a failed parent either. What it simply means is that our kids push back and think for themselves. And sometimes what seems to you to be the worst-case scenario can end up with your child's making a deeper commitment to the Lord.

The familiar story of the prodigal son in Luke 15 is one of the most beautiful pieces of literature in all of the world. Both Charles Dickens and Ralph Waldo Emerson stated that it was probably the greatest short story ever written. But it's more than great literature; it's a story Jesus told that shows us how we often run from God. But it's also a story that shows us what we ought to do as Christian parents when our children rebel:

> A certain man had two sons. And the younger of them said to his father, 'Father, give me the portion of goods that falls to me.' So he divided to them his livelihood. And not many days after, the younger son gathered all together, journeyed to a far country, and there wasted his possessions with prodigal living. But when he had spent all, there arose a severe famine in that land, and he began to be in want. Then he went and joined himself to a citizen of that country, and he sent him into his fields to feed swine. And he would gladly have filled his stomach with the pods that the swine ate, and no one gave him anything. (Luke 15:11-16)

What can we observe from this passage? The boy simply wanted independence from his father.

In verse 12, the son says, "Give me the portion of goods that falls to me." In Jewish law at this time, the oldest son would receive two-thirds of the inheritance, and the rest was divided among the younger children. As the youngest of two sons, this young man wanted his third right away.

By making this request while his father was still living, he was saying, in effect, "You know what, Dad? I wish you were dead. And, frankly, I'm tired of waiting around for you to die. I want my portion of the inheritance now."

He saw his father as an impediment or restraint in his life, and he wanted complete independence from his home. And this may very well happen with our sons or daughters, too.

We read in verse 13, "The younger son gathered all together." What does that mean? That means he turned everything into cash. There was a vast estate here with servants, hired help, buildings, and land. How do you liquidate something that quickly? You sell it off at a discount. So he took his inheritance and got as much money out of it as he possibly could.

But why did he leave? This appears to have been a wonderful home. There was no abuse here. No mention of divorce or hypocrisy or alcoholic parents or a passive father. In fact, this appears to have been a stable, loving home with a very hands-on dad. It also was a loving, nurturing home, as evidenced by the warm affection the father showed his son when he finally returned.

It was an affluent home, with servants, meaning this boy wanted for nothing growing up. I'm guessing there was faith in this home as well. This would be the sort of dad who would read Scripture to his sons and take them to worship with him.

Nevertheless, the youngest son rejected it all; he wanted to go his own way. In fact, shortly after receiving his inheritance, he took off for a far country. Wherever he landed, I'm sure he must have made quite a splash with all that money to flash around. As soon as his money ran out, however, his friends ran out with it. According to his older brother, he even turned to prostitutes, dragging his good family name through the gutter.

In time, the young rebel discovered the emptiness of life without his father. In verse 14, we read, "When he had spent all, there arose a severe famine in that land, and he began to be in want."

You see, Dad wasn't there to turn to. His whole life he had turned to his dad in times of trouble or pain, but now he was far from home—by his own choice. When crisis hits, we usually turn to family: our spouse, parents, siblings, children, loved ones. But in that far country, this young man had no family to turn to and he was despondent. In desperation, he finally attached himself to a local citizen, asking him for a job—any job. So the man sent him out to feed the pigs.

But all the while, God was at work.

And the boy began to return to his senses.

Sometimes when we're praying our hearts out for our prodigal kids, things suddenly seem to get worse rather than better. Maybe we've been praying, "Lord, bring my son back to You" or "Bring my daughter back to You." And then we hear that he's been thrown out of school, or she's been fired from her job, or there's some new financial crisis. Maybe there's trouble with the law, and your prodigal gets arrested.

You say, "God, where were You when this bad stuff happened to my child?" I will tell you where God was: He was right there, trying to bring the child to his senses. And as we all know, sometimes the only way someone will learn is the hard way. You have to get to the end of yourself before you get to the beginning of God.

Both of my sons had their prodigal years, but Christopher more than Jonathan. He went astray for a number of years.

The young man in Jesus' story had gone astray as well, and I'm sure there were many sleepless nights for this father. But note how the story ends:

> When he came to himself, he said, "How many of my father's hired servants have bread enough and to spare, and I perish with hunger! I will arise and go to my father, and will say to him, 'Father, I have sinned against heaven and before you, and I am no longer worthy to be called your son. Make me like one of your hired servants.'"
>
> And he arose and came to his father. (verses 17-20)

So the weary rebel, the prodigal son, returned home again. He went to the dog, he fed the hogs, and homeward he jogs.

And how does his father react to the homecoming?

> When he was still a great way off, his father saw him and had compassion, and ran and fell on his neck and kissed him. (verse 20)

This would indicate to me that the father was watching for his boy. I have a mental picture of him sitting out on the front porch in his rocker, along toward evening, looking down that long road his son had taken when he left home. Maybe he would look down that winding path into the distance and pray for his boy to come home.

And then one day, he did.

> The son said to him, "Father, I have sinned against heaven and in your sight, and am no longer worthy to be called your son."
>
> But the father said to his servants, "Bring out the best robe and put

> it on him, and put a ring on his hand and sandals on his feet. And bring the fatted calf here and kill it, and let us eat and be merry; for this my son was dead and is alive again; he was lost and is found." And they began to be merry. (verses 21-24)

WHAT DO WE LEARN FROM THIS STORY?

1. Stay true to your beliefs.

Just because your child pushes back doesn't mean you should back down. Hold your course. Live as a good example. Teach the Word to your child. Understand that even if your child goes through a rough patch, it doesn't mean he or she will stay there forever.

We have always had rules in our home, and I would say to my boys, "Listen, if you live under my roof, you live by my rules. And if you break those rules, there are repercussions." Both of my sons understood that. And even though they would disagree with me at times, they were always respectful. Was there tension? Yes, sometimes there was. But that very tension is a good thing if you are standing consistently for what is right and true.

When Christopher came back to the Lord after his period of rebellion, he told one of his friends that he had used me as a kind of barometer. He said, "When I was right with God, I noticed how well I got along with my dad. And when I wasn't right with God, I felt tension between Dad and me."

It was right that he would feel that tension. Why? Because I didn't want to send out the signal that I approved of how he had been living. Even though it wasn't always easy, I needed to hold my ground and stand on my principles.

2. Never give up on them.

Your rebellious son or daughter might escape your presence but can never escape your prayers. And what may seem like a worst-case scenario can be the very thing that brings him or her back to the Lord.

3. Keep the porch light on and leave the door to home open.

When the prodigal son finally came to his senses, he knew he could go home. He knew he could go back to his father no matter what. He knew the porch light would be on and his dad would open the door and bring him inside.

When Christopher was in his prodigal mode, I always kept communication open. Sometimes I wouldn't speak with him for a week or longer, but we would communicate through e-mail or I would call him. We would get together for lunch. And those were uncomfortable meetings at times, but he always knew I loved him.

Finally, the time came when he did make the recommitment to the Lord. And it seemed like he made up for lost time. He got married, his life took off spiritually, and he started a Bible study in his home.

He was doing so well. And three years after he made that recommitment to Christ, he was called home to heaven. Looking back on the way I raised both of my sons, I wouldn't try to tell you that I was a perfect parent, nor am I a perfect parent today. (But I think I'm doing really well as a grandparent!) To be honest, however, I don't have any regrets. I made some mistakes, but I think I did the best that I could, and I consistently leaned on the Lord for strength and wisdom.

Our youngest son, Jonathan (the one who got lost in the elevator), also had his prodigal time. He wasn't like

Christopher, wandering so far away. Jonathan was still at home but was living a double life that we weren't aware of. And then it came to our attention, and we realized that we had not one but two prodigal sons. But he, too, made a recommitment to the Lord.

I asked him to tell his story to our church, and what follows is a transcript of that brief message. I will let Jonathan wrap up this chapter:

> I was born and raised in Southern California, Orange County specifically. I grew to love skateboarding, going to the beach, swimming, and surfing. I was like every other kid. I liked to goof off in class, make jokes, whatever. Sometimes teachers liked to single me out because of who my dad is. They would say, "Oh, Jonathan, I would expect more from you, seeing who your dad is."
>
> When you're a kid, you take that stuff to heart. People are expecting more from you, but I just wanted to blend in and be like everyone else.
>
> Growing up around my mom and dad, I can tell you one thing for sure: I was never able to doubt the existence of God. I recognized they had a true relationship with Jesus Christ. The faith that my dad showed in the pulpit was the same faith he showed in the kitchen at home. He was always the same guy. He has a great love for his family, and I've always known that.
>
> As time went by, I began to resent this question: "Little Jonathan, are you going to grow up to be a preacher like your father?"
>
> I wanted to be known as *Jonathan* Laurie, not as Jonathan *Laurie*, the son of Greg Laurie, the famous pastor and evangelist. I wanted to prove to them and myself that I could be my own person and didn't have to follow in my father's footsteps.
>
> When I was sixteen, a friend persuaded me to try some marijuana

for the first time. We were at his house, in the backyard. I remember being scared.

Six months later, I was getting high three to five times a day, drinking alcohol, and smoking cigarettes. As I continued to live this lifestyle of smoking marijuana and living in my parents' home, I found myself living a double life. I was lying to everybody. The thing was, I couldn't run away from who I was. At parties, my friends would introduce me as Greg Laurie's son.

They would say, "Hey, do you know who this guy's dad is? Have you heard of the Harvest Crusades? Greg Laurie? That's his dad! Have you seen the billboard of the guy on the 55 freeway that's about thirteen feet tall? That's his dad!"

So I kept being identified as the very person I was running from. I think there might be a bit of humor there on God's part.

I successfully lied to my parents for about a year. When I was seventeen, I was in a parking lot down in Newport with friends. We were standing around my car in the parking lot at 11:00 on a Friday night, smoking pot. Not the smartest place in the world to do illicit drugs! Well, sure enough, a cop car rolls up and he busts us. I get arrested for possession of marijuana. My parents had no idea. I had to come and tell them point blank what I had been up to for the past year and a half or so. It was tough.

So as a result, they put me on restriction. They took away my car. No time with my friends. No surfing. No going outside. No skateboarding. Nothing. Just Mom and Dad time.

But before I had told them what happened, I told my brother Christopher. He prayed for me. He encouraged me to seek accountability and get some Christian friends. He told me of his own problems of drug use and lies. He said that it was a lifestyle of temporary fulfillment and that it was empty.

So after a few months of being grounded, I started to get some privileges back. I earned some trust. And what did I do? I immediately went back to those old friends and took up right where I had left off. I never was really fully honest with anybody. But the one person I did share with more than anyone was Christopher.

One day we were driving in the car. He looked over at me, and after I shared some stuff that had been going on in my life, he asked me, "Jonathan, what's it going to take?"

You see, we had been talking about giving my life to Christ, and he asked me what it was going to take. I don't really remember what my response was. I probably blew it off to some degree and said something like, "I'm just having fun, and I'm not hurting anybody. Besides, I've got all the time in the world."

I acted like it was no big deal, but his question really stuck with me.

On a Thursday morning on my job, my boss walked by and asked me how everything was going. He happened to be a friend of our family. I told him everything was going pretty good. And then he showed up again about an hour later with a police officer friend of ours. They told me at that point that I should come with them — that I needed to go home.

When I rounded the corner in our neighborhood, I looked in front of my house and saw my father weeping. Then I saw him collapse on the ground in the front yard. I didn't know what to make of it. As I got out of the car, a friend of ours walked up to me, grabbed me by the shoulder, looked me in the eyes, and told me, "Jonathan, Christopher died."

I felt vacant. I was vacant. I didn't know how to respond to it. My only brother was gone. The only person I was ever truly honest with now wasn't on earth anymore.

After everybody had left our house and things began to settle, I began to wonder what it all meant. Instantly, Christopher's words popped back into my head: *Jonathan, what's it going to take? What's it going to take for you to give your life to Christ?*

I knew what I had to do. I went into my room. I grabbed the drugs, alcohol, pornography, cigarettes, whatever I was still hiding from my parents. (I had all kinds of hiding spots.) I put it all on my bed in front of me and asked Christ to come into my heart. I prayed for Him to forgive me. I prayed for Him to take away the addiction from me and also the desire to do these things. And He has been faithful to do that.

So today I am married to the girl I had a crush on in junior high and high school. My wife and I have two children together, with another one on the way. God has blessed me more than I ever could have imagined. If you had told me six years ago that I would be on video sharing my testimony, that I would be married with two children and another one on the way, I probably would have laughed in your face. But that is what the Lord can do. He can change anybody if you just give Him an open heart. I didn't give my life to Christ because someone wanted me to or didn't want me to; I did it because I wanted the hope of heaven. I wanted the hope of seeing my brother again and being reunited with family and friends. I wanted to see Jesus face-to-face.

As Christians, we have the hope of heaven, not the hope of a life without sadness. You see, God can use these things to bring us closer to Him.

So maybe you are the parent of a prodigal son or a prodigal daughter and you would ask me, "What advice would you give to me?"

I would say this: You need to be praying fervently for your son or daughter. I know that my parents were praying for me, and the Lord answered their prayers. You need to be really on your face, asking for God to save your son or daughter. And He will do it.

You need to have unconditional love. You need to love your child, your son or your daughter, in their sin. That doesn't mean that you approve of what they are doing. But you need to let them know that no matter what, you love them and you will always love them.

Third, and probably most important, you need to live the example. You need to step it up. You need to *show* them that this is not a façade or some act that you're putting on but that it's a true thing in your heart that you have convictions about. They will recognize that. They will respect that.

Now, for you prodigals out there (if you are listening right now), I've got this to say to you: It's a waste of time. It is empty, and it leaves quick. That joy that you feel, and as high as you got, that is how *low* you will be the next day. It won't stay with you.

As a Christian now, I can honestly tell you I am happier than I have ever been. I don't have regrets. I don't have to get up in the morning and think, *Oh my gosh, did I really do that last night?* I don't have to worry about getting busted by the police. I don't have to worry about friends dying because of drug abuse. God took those things away. Thank You, Jesus. I don't have to worry about those things anymore. That is a burden lifted off of my shoulders.

I dare you to ask God to make Himself real to you. In Proverbs 8:17, it says, "Those that seek Me . . . will find Me." In the story of the prodigal son, the son was a long way off and the father ran and met him. That means God will meet you where you're at. You don't have to clean up. You don't have to change first. He will help you do that. You need to just give your life to Christ, and He will do the work for you.

So I was a prodigal, my brother was a prodigal, and maybe you are the parent of a prodigal or you're a prodigal yourself. There is hope. We serve a God who does great things. He can change you and your ways right now.

So God bless you, and to God be the glory.

CHAPTER SEVEN

HOPE OF HEAVEN

GEORGE BERNARD SHAW WAS a famous English intellectual, writer, and outspoken atheist who won a Nobel Prize for literature. Shaw, who died in 1950, believed with all his heart that the hope and future of the human race would be ushered in through advances in science and technology.

But at the end of his life, he changed his tune.

Before his death at the age of ninety-four, he wrote these words:

> The science to which I pinned my faith is bankrupt. Its counsels, which should have established a millennium, led instead directly to the suicide of Europe. I believed them once. In their name I helped to destroy the faith of millions of worshipers in the temples of a thousand creeds. And now they look at me and witness the great tragedy of an atheist who lost his faith.[1]

George Bernard Shaw put his faith in the wrong thing. As the old saying goes, he finally reached the top of the ladder, only to discover that the ladder was leaning against the wrong wall and offered no hope at all.

Where have you placed your hope?

HOPE IS MORE THAN WISHING

Different people, of course, define the word *hope* in different ways. Some people think of it as nothing more than something they might wish for and would use the word interchangeably with *fate*, *good luck*, *serendipity*, or maybe *wishing upon a star.*

In the classic Disney cartoon *Pinocchio*, a cricket named Jiminy tried to encourage the little wooden puppet by singing, "When you wish upon a star . . . your dreams come true."

It's a nice thought, but it isn't true.

I hate to break this to you Disney fans, but Jiminy's words just don't hold water. (Never trust a cricket in a top hat.) The fact is, you can wish upon a star all you want, but that won't make anything turn out better. In fact, if that's all you do in a crisis, things probably will get worse.

Sometimes people will put their hope in their investments, bank accounts, stock portfolios, or the home they live in. If you listen much to the radio, you will hear commercial after commercial insisting that buying gold will give you security when all else fails.

But gold is no better than wishing on a star. Not in the long run.

Job 8:13-15 says,

The same happens to all who forget God.
The hopes of the godless evaporate.
Their confidence hangs by a thread.
They are leaning on a spider's web.
They cling to their home for security, but it won't last.
They try to hold it tight, but it will not endure. (NLT)

We should not put our hope in man. We should not put our hope in finances or material possessions. We need to put our hope in God. That is what the Bible teaches. In Psalm 42, the psalmist counseled himself with these words: "Why am I discouraged? Why is my heart so sad? I will put my hope in God! I will praise him again — my Savior and my God!" (verses 5-6, NLT).

Putting hope in our God and Savior will give us the strength to go on in life. Why? Because we know there is an afterlife, where things will be made right.

Believe it or not, that last statement will make some people angry. I came across an atheist website a while back that was very critical of something similar I had written about heaven.

Their response made me happy.

Anytime I say something that angers atheists, I figure I am doing something right. Here is what I had written, to which they took such strong exception: "When a Christian dies, it is a direct flight to heaven. There are no stopovers. The moment we take our last breath on earth, we will take our first breath in heaven. We go into the presence of God."

Here is how the atheists responded: "Going to heaven after death is assumed. Not only does Laurie start with this unsubstantiated and onerous assumption, but then he goes on in more detail about the precise state of affairs that take place in heaven once you arrive. And what evidence is offered to bolster these claims? Nothing at all. Just a bunch of Bible quotes."

I don't expect atheists to understand the hope of a Christian, but I would also say this: This hope to which we cling is neither wishful thinking nor blind optimism. It is quiet confidence, and it is a supernatural certainty. And where do we find this hope? We find it in the pages of Scripture—or, as the atheists would say, in "just a bunch of Bible quotes."

TRUE AND LASTING HOPE

True and lasting hope comes from God and His Word. One of the reasons Scripture was given to us in the first place was so that we might have hope. Paul said as much in Romans 15:4: "Such things were written in the Scriptures long ago to teach us. And the Scriptures give us hope and encouragement as we wait patiently for God's promises to be fulfilled" (NLT).

It's very important for us to understand what the Bible means when it speaks of hope. It is not the hope of this world. It is not some weak, wishful, think-positive, Pollyanna kind of thing. No, it is altogether different from that. Biblical hope speaks of *certainties*. True biblical hope is a strong and confident expectation.

I can't explain it to you. I just know that I possess it. Perhaps you do as well. And if you want to know under what circumstances this hope will grow stronger, I'll tell you (but you might not believe me). It will grow stronger in crisis.

It is one thing to talk about all of this as theory, but it's quite another to put these concepts to the test in the push-and-pull of real life.

I'm here to tell you that I have done that.

I have put my faith to the test; I have taken the promises of God for a test-drive. And they have performed with beauty and power. Again and again, I have had it confirmed to me that all of those things I have been preaching and teaching for so many years are completely true.

That's very reassuring to me. I don't know whether it's reassuring to you, but you don't have to build your faith on what I tell you in this book. You, too, have the promises of God from His Word and can put them to the test yourself.

Why is it so important to make sure of your hope? Because things don't always work out so well in life. Just within the pages of this book, we have spoken of those who have lost loved ones, faced numerous crises, and endured the long agony of a prodigal child.

Sometimes God, in His grace, will turn those situations around. But, honestly, there are times when things don't work out as we had hoped.

That marriage unravels and never comes back together.

That prodigal child doesn't contact you.

That single person never finds a mate.

That person in crisis doesn't have the happy resolution he or she was hoping for.

That person who prayed for physical healing didn't experience it.

What then? What is our response? Should we give up hope? Not at all! When those difficult things happen, we are compelled to remember that both the wonders and the heartaches of this life are only temporary.

We make so much of this life: preserving it, holding on to it, propping it up, trying to enhance it. But the fact is that no matter how long we might live, life comes and goes rather quickly. The Bible says in 1 Chronicles 29:15, "We are here for only a moment, visitors and strangers in the land as our ancestors were before us. Our days on earth are like a passing shadow, gone so soon without a trace" (NLT).

We think far too much about this life and not enough about the next one. In his book *We Shall See God,* Randy Alcorn wrote,

> Eternal life means enjoying forever the finest moments of life on Earth the way they were intended. Since in Heaven we'll finally experience life at its best, it would be more accurate to call our present existence the *beforelife* rather than to call what follows the *afterlife.*[2]

That's a great thought. We talk about the afterlife, but here we are living in the "beforelife." And it flies by very quickly.

I'm reminded of going to the movies and watching the previews before the movie starts. You don't go to the theater to watch a preview; you go to see the movie itself. In many ways, life on earth is like the previews that flit by so quickly, and the film is eternity, the main event.

Every person who has ever lived will live eternally. A human being is a living soul made in the image of God, and we will all live on beyond this life, whether we believe in God or don't believe in God. The bigger question is *where* we will spend eternity. If you are a Christian, the answer to that question is heaven. If you are not a Christian, the Bible says that when you die, you will be separated from God forever in hell.

WHEN WRONGS WILL BE RIGHTED

We've all experienced the truth that life isn't fair and that it's filled with inequities and injustice. Certainly, there are times when good is rewarded and bad is punished, but far too often we see the very opposite happen: We see good people suffer and evil people succeed. But although it's true that life isn't fair, it's also true that God is good. He is also righteous and holy, and He loves all of us.

One day in eternity, God will right all wrongs. All of those unanswered questions will be dealt with, and the unfair happenings of life will be resolved. Pain will be replaced by comfort, and tears will be replaced by joy and laughter. In heaven, all of the losses and sorrows will be more than compensated for. Remembering this will give us a better perspective on the struggles of life.

In 2 Corinthians 4:17-18, Paul wrote,

> Our present troubles are small and won't last very long. Yet they produce for us a glory that vastly outweighs them and will last forever! So we don't look at the troubles we can see now; rather, we fix our gaze on things that cannot be seen. For the things we see now will soon be gone, but the things we cannot see will last forever. (NLT)

Right now, we see things in a certain way, but that can change overnight. And that change can happen in a nanosecond when we enter into eternity.

In Luke 16, Jesus gives us a classic example of this in the story of the rich man and Lazarus, the beggar. Some people refer to this story as a "parable," or one of the illustrations Jesus would use to make His point. But it doesn't read like a parable at all to me because He actually names Lazarus, something He doesn't do in His parables.

Jesus began the story by describing the lifestyle of a certain wealthy man who wore the finest clothing, lived in a beautiful mansion, and had servants at his beck and call. We can imagine him living the high life, with big parties every week. Right outside the gates of his estate, an impoverished and desperately ill man named Lazarus was put every day to beg for money or food. Literally starving, Lazarus would long to eat just a few scraps from the rich man's table.

The sin of the rich man wasn't that he was rich; his sin was that he lived only for his personal pleasures, had no place in his life for God, and had no compassion for the plight of a dying man who had been placed at his very gate.

Then both men passed into eternity. No doubt the rich man had a big funeral, with his picture in the paper. Lazarus probably was buried in an unmarked grave, just to get his body off the street. And seemingly no one cared. The Bible tells us, however, that one went to a place of comfort and the other went to a place of torment. And just that quickly, the rich man and Lazarus traded places, and everything was different.

As Dinesh D'Souza said, heaven is the venue of cosmic justice. In other words, it will all be sorted out on the other side.

Heaven is the opportunity to develop and fulfill dreams bigger than anything on this earth. We must recognize that even if you didn't accomplish something you deeply desired to accomplish on earth, you may be able to accomplish it—or something much greater—later on, either in heaven or on the new earth when we rule and reign with Jesus Christ.

This is so important to realize because good people on this side of heaven sometimes have very difficult lives or even lives that are cut short. I can't think of anything sadder than when a child dies or a young man or woman leaves us in what we would perceive to be before their time. Or maybe we'll see a person who has to navigate this life with a severe disability and it just seems to us as though he or she has lost out in life or gotten the short end of the stick.

God, however, promises to compensate for the difficult or painful years we experience in this life. In eternity, He will allow us to realize our dreams and fulfill our potential. Death for the believer is not the end of life but rather the continuation of it in another place.

We will be better off eternally because we suffered temporarily.

We think of the here and now; God thinks of the by-and-by. We think of the temporal; God thinks of the eternal. We think about what will make us happy; God thinks about what will make us holy. He looks at the big picture.

So in this plan and purpose of God for my life, there may be things I have gone through and had to endure that make no sense at all to me now. But when I get to heaven, I will realize I became a better person for it. I was shaped more and more into the image of Jesus Christ as a result of it. I will look back on those hardships and trials and say, "Now I understand why God allowed that to happen to me."

I think the argument for "the greater good" may be the strongest biblical case for why God allows suffering in our lives. But this takes faith—and patience—because we can't see that "good" right now. In fact, I may not see the good in all my days on earth.

But someday, in heaven, I will.

My hope is built on a sure foundation: the hope of heaven itself.

PREWIRED WITH HOPE

In Colossians 1:5, Paul speaks of the "faith and love that spring from the hope that is stored up for you in heaven" (NIV).

You and I have been prewired with hope. There is a restless yearning in the human heart for something more than this world can offer. As Augustine said, "You formed us for yourself, and our hearts are restless until they find their rest in You."

The truth is, I never will find quite what I am looking for in *anything* this world has to offer. In Romans 8, it says that I groan inwardly for the redemption of my body, and it is in this hope that I am saved.

Have you ever read about the amazing little bird known as the golden plover? This is a bird with incredible homing instincts. Native to Hawaii, the plover migrates during the summer to the Aleutian Isles, which are 1,200 miles away. There they mate, they lay their eggs, and their little fledglings are born. After that, the golden plovers return to the airways and cruise back to Hawaii.

How can this creature fly from Hawaii to the Aleutian Isles and back to Hawaii again with no maps, no MapQuest directions, no compass, and no GPS? They just do it, relying on homing instincts built into their little bird brains by God Himself.

In the same way, God has given to me and to you a homing instinct for a place we have never been before. The little plover has never been to Hawaii, yet somehow it knows how to get there. And even though you have never been to heaven, you long for heaven because it is your true home. This is what the Bible is talking about when it says that God has set eternity in our hearts (see Ecclesiastes 3:11). We have a heavenly GPS built into our eternal spirits.

C. S. Lewis calls this yearning for heaven "the inconsolable longing." Speaking of this longing, he writes, "It is the secret signature of each soul. The incommunicable and unappeasable want."[3]

Until that day we arrive in heaven, we live between two coexisting worlds.

Even though there are all kinds of books in the Christian marketplace about people who claim to have been to heaven and have come back again, the only true word about heaven we really have is in the Bible itself.

God has given us one Book to tell us about heaven. Scripture speaks of a supernatural world that surrounds us at this very moment. I tend to believe that heaven isn't as far away as we might think. We may envision heaven as someplace impossibly far away, tucked in the corner of a distant galaxy, but the Bible never actually says that heaven is distant. In fact, there may be only the thinnest of veils between us and the afterlife.

The Bible also tells us that we are surrounded by angels. In Psalm 34:7, we're told that "the angel of the LORD encamps all around those who fear Him, and delivers them." These heavenly beings are actively involved in doing the work of God in our lives. The New Testament says that angels are "spirit-messengers sent out to help and care for those who are to receive his salvation" (Hebrews 1:14, TLB).

In the Old Testament, we read the story of the prophet Elisha, who was with his servant in an Israelite town called Dothan. While they were there, an army of enemy Aramean soldiers surrounded the town, intent on apprehending the prophet:

> One night the king of Aram sent a great army with many chariots and horses to surround the city.
>
> When the servant of the man of God got up early the next morning and went outside, there were troops, horses, and chariots everywhere. "Oh, sir, what will we do now?" the young man cried to Elisha.
>
> "Don't be afraid!" Elisha told him. "For there are more on our side than on theirs!" Then Elisha prayed, "O LORD, open his eyes and let him see!" The LORD opened the young man's eyes, and when he looked up, he saw that the hillside around Elisha was filled with horses and chariots of fire. (2 Kings 6:14-17, NLT)

The prophet's servant was allowed a glimpse of the unseen angelic armies of God.

Can you imagine how a glimpse like that would change the way we think? It would change our priorities, it would help us look at our problems in a new way, and it would certainly give us more hope.

In the book of Acts, Stephen, the church's first martyr, would be another example of someone "between two worlds." He, too, was given a glimpse of the reality beyond this earth just before being mobbed and stoned to death for his faith in Jesus:

> He, being full of the Holy Spirit, gazed into heaven and saw the glory of God, and Jesus standing at the right hand of God, and said, "Look! I see the heavens opened and the Son of Man standing at the right hand of God!" (Acts 7:55-56)

As the stones were hurled, crushing the life out of this young man, he prayed, "Lord Jesus, receive my spirit" (verse 59).

In that moment, Stephen had a foot in each world, heaven and earth.

To one degree or another, this can happen to you and me, too. Sometimes it takes a severe crisis to open our eyes to the eternal world—perhaps a brush with death or the passing of a loved one. More than ever before, we find ourselves thinking about the next world, and, in a sense, we start living in two worlds. In other words, we're made aware of eternity; we begin thinking in the light of eternity and planning our lives accordingly.

In the beforelife, we need to be thinking more about the afterlife.

"SET YOUR HEARTS"

In Colossians 3:1-3, Paul wrote, "Since, then, you have been raised with Christ, set your hearts on things above, where Christ is seated at the right hand of God. Set your minds on things above, not on earthly things. For you died, and your life is now hidden with Christ in God" (NIV).

What does that mean? What does it mean to set your heart and mind on things above? To "set your mind" means to engage in a diligent, active, single-minded investigation.

In other words, think about heaven more.

What's more, the verb in this verse is in the present tense, so it could be translated "keep thinking about heaven." Paul is telling us to constantly keep seeking and thinking about heaven.

We truly are people of two worlds, with our feet on earth and our minds in heaven. Sadly, however, some of us will go all day—or all month—without a single thought of heaven or eternity. But if we are living as we ought to live as Christians, we *will* think about it.

You say, "How can I think about a place I've never been before?"

Answer: by thinking about what the Bible says about heaven and how it should affect our lives.

Maybe heaven to you is something vague or misty—more of a state of mind than a tangible piece of real estate.

According to Scripture, however, heaven is an actual place. It is the dwelling place of God Himself. In John 14:2-3, Jesus said, "There is more than enough room in my Father's home. If this were not so, would I have told you that I am going to prepare a place for you? When everything is ready, I will come and get you, so that you will always be with me where I am" (NLT).

How clear is that?

Jesus is preparing a place for us—a place where we can be with Him.

I think one of the problems is that through the years, we develop a caricatured version of heaven in our minds. It's a combination of movies, TV shows, cartoons, and bad sermons. It all melds in our imaginations to give us a picture of a weird, misty place where people in robes sit on clouds and strum harps.

And, frankly, it's a picture that looks pretty boring. We can't imagine being there for a week, let alone an eternity. But that's the cartoon heaven, not the real one. Biblical heaven is different altogether.

DESCRIPTIVE WORDS

The Bible uses different words to describe this place we call heaven.

1. Heaven is a paradise.

Paul the apostle had the unique experience of actually dying, going to heaven, and coming back again. Interestingly, he didn't write a book about it. He could have written a whole New Testament epistle about heaven and all the things he saw and heard. But he chose not to. Even if the Lord had permitted him to speak about what he experienced, I think he would have been at a loss for words.

Here is how he describes the events surrounding that visit:

> I know a man who, fourteen years ago, was seized by Christ and swept in ecstasy to the heights of heaven. I really don't know if this took place in the body or out of it; only God knows. I also know that this man was hijacked into paradise — again, whether in or out of the body, I don't

> know; God knows. There he heard the unspeakable spoken, but was forbidden to tell what he heard. (2 Corinthians 12:2-4, MSG)

He used one word to describe it: paradise.

That is a very hard word to translate. Jesus used the same term with the thief on the cross when that man said to Him, "Jesus, remember me when you come into your kingdom."

And Jesus answered him, "I tell you the truth, today you will be with me in paradise" (Luke 23:42-43, NIV).

It's a word used to describe the walled gardens of a king. Most of us have never visited such a place. The closest we could come to describing it would be the immaculately kept gardens of some fabulous estate.

Paul was saying, "It was like that, but I really don't want to say any more."

All we know is that heaven was way better than earth, as Paul—who had been there—said in Philippians, "What shall I choose? I do not know! I am torn between the two: I desire to depart and be with Christ, which is better by far" (Philippians 1:22-23, NIV).

In the Greek language, Paul used a superlative form of *better*, which means *way* better or, as they would say in Hawaii, "Mo better, bra."

Nobody in heaven, if given the choice, would ever want to come back to earth again. But Paul went to heaven and had to return.

I like to try to imagine the conversation Paul had with the Lord when he arrived in heaven during that brief stay.

Paul says, "Wow! Am I really here?"

And the Lord replies, "Welcome, Paul. Well done. I've

got some good news and some bad news for you."

"Lord, what do You mean good news and bad news? What's the good news?"

"You will be coming back here again."

"Coming *back again*? Am I going somewhere?"

"Yes, and that brings Me to the bad news. You have to go back to earth again."

"Oh, no! Why?"

"Because there is a group of believers standing around your body, and they are praying for you to be raised from the dead."

"Lord, don't listen to them. I don't want to leave. I want to stay here."

"I know, Paul. But I actually have work for you to do down there, so I want you to return for a time. In a few years, you'll be back here again with Me."

Meanwhile, back on earth, the believers are standing around the beaten, bloodied body of Paul, who had just been stoned and left for dead. Suddenly, as they are praying, a flush of color returns to the apostle's face. His chest heaves, his eyes blink, and he gets to his feet.

I think if I had been Paul, I would have felt like hitting someone! But no, Paul got up and went right back to work again, pursuing the mission God had given him to accomplish. Nevertheless, in his brief experience of the Other Side, he described it as a paradise.

2. Heaven is a city.

Hebrews 11:10 speaks of looking forward to the heavenly city, "the city with foundations, whose architect and builder is God" (NIV). The writer went on to say, "Here we have no continuing city, but we the seek the one to come" (Hebrews 13:14).

D. L. Moody once said that heaven is as real a place as Chicago. He was right. We need to get away from this idea of some foggy, mystical, dreamy netherworld and realize that heaven is a city—a real city.

What do we know about cities? There are things to do, places to go, and activities to get involved in, right? You have culture, music, architecture, stores, and places to eat.

Am I saying that such things will be in heaven?

I don't know. I just know that the Bible says heaven is a city.

We've all seen things that we don't like in cities—urban decay, trash, crime, and so forth. But don't think of those things; think of the best, most beautiful city you've ever visited. Think of Jerusalem at sunrise, Rome at sunset, a castle on a green hill in Ireland.

No, heaven won't be anything like those places, but it is a place—a paradise, a city. But that's not all.

3. Heaven is a country.

> All these people died still believing what God had promised them. They did not receive what was promised, but they saw it all from a distance and welcomed it. They agreed that they were foreigners and nomads here on earth. Obviously people who say such things are looking forward to a country they can call their own. If they had longed for the country they came from, they could have gone back. But they were looking for a better place, a heavenly homeland. That is why God is not ashamed to be called their God, for he has prepared a city for them. (Hebrews 11:13-16, NLT)

Don't you love that? A country we can call our own . . . a better place . . . a heavenly homeland . . . a city. Those of us who have trusted Jesus Christ for salvation are headed to a real place, an authentic destination.

Those thoughts alone are enough to fill me up with wonder. But there is so much more:

> I saw a new heaven and a new earth, for the old heaven and the old earth had disappeared. And the sea was also gone. And I saw the holy city, the new Jerusalem, coming down from God out of heaven like a bride beautifully dressed for her husband. (Revelation 21:1-2, NLT)

A new heaven *and* a new earth? What an amazing thing to think about! And then that glorious heavenly city, descending to a brand-new world so that heaven and earth effectively become one!

Think of a whole new earth to explore as well as a vast, incredibly beautiful city, the New Jerusalem. All the believers of all ages will be together and—best of all—will be with the Lord forever. These are firm promises for children of God. This is why we have hope in a hopeless world.

What are you facing? What is troubling you right now? Do you feel hopeless? I hope not. You can feel helpless at times, but don't ever feel *hopeless*. There is always hope, and that hope is in a God who loves you and never changes. In His great grace and kindness, your situation might be resolved and your circumstances might change for the better.

But even if they don't, you still have the ultimate hope that one day you will be with the Lord.

And that thought should put everything else in perspective.

CHAPTER EIGHT

HOPE FOR
TROUBLED HEARTS
THOSE WHO LOST LOVED ONES
THOSE WHO GRIEVE
THOSE FACING CRISIS
FAILING MARRIAGES

THE BLESSED HOPE

A PASTOR WHO WAS speaking on the topic of heaven asked his congregation, "How many of you would like to go to heaven tonight?"

Everybody raised their hand except one little boy up in the balcony.

So the pastor asked the question again. "Again I ask you, how many of you would like to go to heaven tonight?" Every hand shot up, with the exception of that boy. So the minister actually singled the little guy out and said, "Son, don't you want to go to heaven?"

The little boy said, "Yeah, I want to go to heaven, but I thought you were getting up a load right now."

We like the idea of going to heaven, but we're not necessarily in a rush to get there. As country artist Kenny Chesney sings, "Everybody wants to go to heaven, but nobody wants to go now."

Younger people reading this chapter might say, "Greg, that's a good message for older people—in their forties and beyond—but I'm still pretty young, so I'm not really thinking about this too much."

The trouble with that thinking is that no one knows when his or her life will end. No one knows when we will step from time into eternity. Pick up the newspaper, and you'll read about way too many young adults, teenagers, and children who have tragically and unexpectedly left this life because of accidents, illnesses, or violence. You never know when your last day, hour, or minute on earth might be.

But here's something else to think about. There is more than one way of getting to heaven. Death is one way, but it isn't the only way. There is a great event on the horizon, perhaps nearer than any of us imagine, which we could all experience together. It's an event the Bible calls "the blessed hope."

I'm speaking, of course, of the rapture of the church, when we will be caught up to meet the Lord in the air. The apostle Paul spoke of this event in Titus 2:13, saying we should be "looking for the blessed hope and glorious appearing of our great God and Savior Jesus Christ."

THE TEACHING THAT CHANGES EVERYTHING

If we understand this biblical teaching about the imminent return of Christ, it should affect the way we live. The apostle John wrote, "We know that when He is revealed, we shall be like Him, for we shall see Him as He is. And everyone who has this hope in Him purifies himself, just as He is pure" (1 John 3:2-3).

In other words, if you really believe this, it should impact the way you live your life. But most of all, it should give you hope.

When we talk about "the hope of heaven," it isn't wishful thinking or blind optimism; it is a supernatural certainty. We know deep in our hearts that we are truly children of God. In Romans 8:16, the apostle tells us, "The Spirit Himself bears witness with our spirit that we are children of God."

Do you have that sense inside of you right now? What a difference that strong assurance can make in our lives—this anticipation that we will meet the Lord one day.

WHAT IS HOPE?

When we use that simple word, what do we really mean by it? Here is an acronym, H-O-P-E, that may help you to better understand hope:

Holding
On with
Patient
Expectation

When we put that all together, we have *hope*.

This principle of hope applies to all of life: when you are facing a crisis, when you have a marriage that is unraveling, when you have a child who has gone prodigal, when you are facing great financial need and don't know where the provision will come from. Whatever crisis you may be facing, you need to exercise biblical hope, which means holding on with patient expectation.

It means holding on to the truth that God is in control of your life even when events seem random and out of control to you. It means believing He can work all things together for good in your life even when you can't see any good at all. It means having faith in a loving heavenly Father who has a watchful eye on your life.

Knowing that the Lord could come back to earth at any moment fills us with hopeful expectation. It's an expectation of seeing Him face-to-face, and it's an expectation of beginning a new life in heaven.

As we said in the previous chapter, heaven is the dwelling place of God Himself. Heaven is a place, not just an idea or a state of mind. Before He left this earth, Jesus said, "In My Father's house are many mansions [or dwelling places]; if it were not so, I would have told you. I go to prepare a place for you" (John 14:2-3).

The Bible says that God has placed eternity in our hearts (see Ecclesiastes 3:11), and sometimes we find ourselves homesick for heaven, a place we have never seen and a home we haven't yet entered.

As Dorothy said to Toto, "There's no place like home." She was right. Anytime you have to be away, you look forward to being home again. Why? Because at home you are comfortable, you're with family, and you can be yourself. Home is a safe, relaxed place.

We even have that notion in the game of baseball. What's the objective of the game? Hopefully, it's to hit a home run—or to at least round the bases and finally slide toward home.

That is what we're thinking about here. For the believer, going to heaven is really going home.

COMMONLY ASKED QUESTIONS

Will we know one another in heaven? This question is asked all the time, but I'm not sure why. Why would I know less in heaven, in the presence of Christ, in my eternal body than I would know here on earth? Listen, when you get to heaven, you will know *more*, not less.

Do you recognize people on earth? Sometimes we don't. Maybe someone will come up to me, such as an old friend or someone I just talked to yesterday, and say, "Greg, how's it going?"

I smile and join in the conversation, all the while hoping I'll get some clue about who the person is, as it's really embarrassing to say, "I'm really sorry, but I've forgotten your name."

Our ability to recognize people on earth can be a little iffy sometimes, but we won't have problems like that in heaven. We will know more there—much more—than we know here. The Bible says in 1 Corinthians 13:12 that "I shall know just as I also am known." Now we see through a glass, sort of like a tinted window, and it's difficult to make things out sometimes. But on the Other Side, everything will be crystal clear. It will be like going from the worst signal imaginable on a forty-year-old TV to the most vivid 3D HD in the world. We will see so many things more clearly than we have ever seen them before.

Will we know each other? A thousand times yes.

Scientists tell us that we use about 5 percent of our brain

capacity (and I can't help but wonder if some people even use the whole 5 percent). In heaven, however, we'll get to use that other 95 percent and probably a lot more as well.

We will recognize one another, and we will still love one another. You will still love your friends, but it will be with stronger, sweeter, purer love. Death breaks ties on earth, but it renews them in heaven. Why? Because heaven will be the perfecting of the highest moments of the present Christian experience.

If you have loved ones in heaven, as I do, you can't help wonder how much they know or don't know about what is going on here on earth. Are residents in heaven completely oblivious to what is happening in our lives today, or do they have ringside seats and watch what happens to us with great interest?

Somehow, I don't think either of those scenarios is correct. I don't think those living in heaven are oblivious to the activities of earth, nor do I think they are necessarily watching our every movement. But I do believe that people in heaven have some level of awareness about what's happening down here.

Let me give you several scriptural illustrations to prove my point.

1. People in eternity are aware of the fact that loved ones are not saved.

In the previous chapter, we looked at Luke 16, which contains the story of the godly beggar, Lazarus, and his rich but uncaring neighbor. You will remember that both of these men passed into eternity—the rich man to a place of torment and Lazarus to a place of comfort. And the rich man who was in torment made this statement: "Please, Father Abraham, at least send him to my father's home. For I have five brothers, and I want him to warn them so they don't end up in this place of torment" (Luke16:27-28, NLT).

This passage seems to indicate that there may be some level of knowledge in eternity about the happenings here on earth.

2. When people believe in Jesus on earth, it is public knowledge in heaven. In Luke 15, Jesus told three parables, all dealing with lost things: a shepherd who had lost a sheep, a woman who had lost a coin, and a father who had lost a son. In the case of the shepherd, we read this:

> What man of you, having a hundred sheep, if he loses one of them, does not leave the ninety-nine in the wilderness, and go after the one which is lost until he finds it? And when he has found it, he lays it on his shoulders, rejoicing. And when he comes home, he calls together his friends and neighbors, saying to them, "Rejoice with me, for I have found my sheep which was lost!" I say to you that likewise there will be more joy in heaven over one sinner who repents than over ninety-nine just persons who need no repentance. (Luke 15:4-7)

So that means that when a person believes on earth, it's a big deal in heaven. (And if it's a big deal in heaven, shouldn't it also be a big deal on earth?)

Sometimes at our Harvest Crusades, we will invite people who want to receive Jesus to come forward. Time after time, I have seen the entire area in front of the stage or platform filled with people. It is always moving. And, frankly, if you ever become jaded to that sort of thing, something isn't right with you spiritually. Your heart should leap every time someone comes to faith.

But there might be another time when we invite people to Christ and perhaps only a handful respond. Maybe we'll go back to the hotel that night thinking, *Well, it didn't go so well tonight.* But wait a second. If one of those seven or eight people who came to Christ that night was your mother or your husband or your child, it would be a very big deal to you. In the same way, it's a hugely important event to God (as it should be to us) when a man or woman, boy or girl receives eternal salvation in Christ. Heaven rejoices when people come to faith.

Then Jesus talks about a woman who lost a coin. "A coin?" we might say. "That's no big deal." In those days, however, instead of a wedding ring, a woman would wear a wedding headband. And in the headband, there were coins. Losing a coin from the headband, then, would be equivalent to losing your wedding ring. So she searched diligently until she found it. Commenting on that incident, Jesus said, "In the same way, there is joy in the presence of God's angels when even one sinner repents" (Luke 15:10, NLT).

Notice how Jesus said, "There is joy *in the presence* of God's angels." It doesn't say there is joy among the angels. In fact, the angels probably do rejoice when someone comes to Christ. But the wording here makes me wonder if the joy referred to here is among the residents of heaven, those who have already passed from this world into the presence of God.

That makes sense, doesn't it? If I know more in heaven than I know on earth, I would surely hear about it if a party broke out among the angels, right? I would want to join in the festivities.

Have you ever been in a room next door to a party? A number of years ago, we did a crusade in San Jose. After the first night's event, we went to our hotel to get some sleep. That's when the party broke out in the next room with loud—really loud—music. I could hear the thump, thump, thump of the bass; in fact, the wall was actually vibrating. So I called security and said, "I don't know what's going on in the room next to me, but you guys have got to come up here. I can't sleep." So they came up, checked, and ended up evicting all the people in the room.

Apparently, it was a bachelor party, and they had hired two DJs with full-blown sound systems. As they were taking the people out of the room, I watched the proceedings in my pajamas, looking out through that little peephole in the door. I saw them carrying out speakers and lighting equipment. Can you imagine?

The point is, I knew there was a party going on. So when I'm in heaven and a celebration breaks out because someone on earth has come to Christ, why wouldn't I be aware of that? Maybe I will have had the opportunity to play a part in that individual's decision to receive Christ. Maybe I will find out that a seed I sowed years ago has finally sprouted and taken root. What a happy moment that would be! Or maybe it will be a son or daughter or grandchild and I will say, "Oh, Lord, how good You are! You let me play a part in that!" I would definitely want to celebrate alongside God's angels.

3. In the book of Revelation, the martyrs watch events on earth.

In Revelation 6:9-11, we read these words:

> When He opened the fifth seal, I saw under the altar the souls of those who had been slain for the word of God and for the testimony which they held.

> And they cried with a loud voice, saying, "How long, O Lord, holy and true, until You judge and avenge our blood on those who dwell on the earth?" Then a white robe was given to each of them; and it was said to them that they should rest a little while longer, until both the number of their fellow servants and their brethren, who would be killed as they were, was completed.

These are believers who have been martyred for their faith during the Tribulation period on earth and have gone to heaven. Notice that although they are in heaven, they have a keen interest in what is still happening on earth. They know they were killed for following Jesus, and they know that God Himself will avenge their blood. This shows a direct continuity between our identity on earth and in heaven. These people are the same people who were slain on earth. They aren't different people; they have simply been relocated!

I have heard it said that we almost become different people in heaven, but that is not the picture I see in Scripture. No, I still will be me. I will be a *perfected* Greg Laurie, but I still will be Greg Laurie—and in a sense, more Greg Laurie than I have ever been.

Some people will say, "I don't see how we could be aware of what's happening on earth when we're in heaven. The Bible says there will be no more sorrow or weeping in heaven. Doesn't it say 'the former things have passed away' in Revelation 21:4?"

Yes, but that doesn't mean you will have had a lobotomy, or a "brain wipe," as in the movie *Men in Black*. You still will be you, you will know more (not less) than you knew on earth, and you will remember things.

"But how can you be aware of sad stuff happening on earth and still enjoy heaven?"

The answer is this: You will have perspective. You will have *heaven's* perspective, and that will make all the difference.

Remember when you were a kid and something traumatic happened and you thought it was the end of your world? The other day, one of my granddaughters came to me in great distress because the head had fallen off her Barbie doll. I tried to fix it, but I couldn't get that head of Barbie's to stay on her shoulders. So what did I do? I told my granddaughter that it would be okay and that I would buy her another Barbie doll or a Disney princess or something else very nice. And she was happy with that. Her perspective had changed.

I remember getting into a fight when I was in elementary school. Actually, it wasn't much of a fight. I got beaten up! As I got off the bus at the bus stop, a bully jumped me. He knocked me onto the ground and was trying to beat my head in. Everyone kept yelling, "Make Laurie eat dirt! Make Laurie eat dirt!" (I might have eaten a little.)

Right after it happened, I felt as though my world had ended. I had nightmares about the whole thing for weeks. What was worse, I was humiliated. Kids laughed at me. It was awful.

But then again, maybe not so awful.

I can look back on the incident now with no pain at all. In fact, it's kind of a funny story to me. At the time it was happening to me, however, it was like Armageddon and it wasn't funny at all. But now I am (much) older and have perspective.

I'm not suggesting that what you may be going through

right now isn't painful or hard. But someday in your wonderful future, when you are looking back at this season of life from the perspective of heaven, in your glorified body, you will see things as God sees them. Your earthly pains and struggles will look much different to you.

Note also that the martyrs in heaven are aware of the passage of time on earth. They say, "How long, O Lord, holy and true, until You judge and avenge our blood on those who dwell on the earth?" (verse 10). How can you be aware of time when you are living outside of time in eternity? I don't know. I just know that these martyrs asked, "How long, O Lord?" They were waiting for something to happen.

A GLORIFIED BODY

Will you and I receive our glorified, made-to-live-forever bodies immediately after we die? I think the answer is no. As I understand the Scriptures, we will receive that new body at the Rapture. The Bible says that the dead in Christ will rise first and we who are alive and remain will be caught up together with them in the cloud, where we will meet the Lord. That is when our mortality will put on immortality and our corruption will put on incorruption (see 1 Thessalonians 4:15-18; 1 Corinthians 15:53).

If we die and go to heaven before that time, what kind of bodies will we have? I don't know. Perhaps there is some kind of intermediate state, with the upgraded, perfected version of the body still to come.

I'm definitely not worried about it. Whatever the Lord provides will be better than I could ever imagine in a billion years. Very soon, however, I know that we will receive our brand-new body. That is great to know, especially when you feel the telltale signs of old age beginning to kick in. Maybe you know what I mean: You don't remember the things you used to remember, and you can't do the things you used to do.

I'm sure you've heard all those "You know you're getting old when . . ." jokes:

- You know you're getting old when your spouse goes out and you don't care where she goes, as long as you don't have to go.
- You know you're getting old when happy hour is a nap.
- You know you're getting old when your idea of weightlifting is standing up.
- You know you're getting old when someone compliments you on your new alligator shoes and you're not wearing shoes.
- You know you're getting old when your knees buckle and your belt won't.

There are a million of them. The point is that a brand-new, forever-youthful body starts to sound better and better as the years slip by.

Some people imagine they will be a wispy, disembodied spirit in heaven. In fact, a poll was taken of Americans who believe in the resurrection of the dead, and two-thirds believe they won't have bodies after the resurrection.

What? Are we all going to be a bunch of ghosts floating around? No. The Bible teaches that we will have a body, and it will be directly connected to the body we're in right now.

Job said, "After my skin is destroyed, this I know, that in my flesh I shall see God" (Job 19:26).

Do you want to know the prototype for this new body? It is Jesus Christ Himself.

The Bible says, "Now we are children of God; and it has not yet been revealed what we shall be, but we know that when He is revealed, we shall be like Him, for we shall see Him as He is" (1 John 3:2). This means that we can take some cues from the resurrected Lord about the body that God has for us in the future. When Jesus rose from the dead, He had a real body in a real world. He had a real voice and a real physical touch. He invited Thomas to touch His hands and side. He ate a piece of fish in their presence.

That brings us to the remarkable scene painted for us in John 21. Let me set the scene just a little. Jesus had been crucified and raised from the dead. He made a number of appearances already to His disciples, including Simon Peter. He had told the disciples to wait for Him, but Peter got tired of waiting. He hung a sign on his office door that said, "Gone fishing."

Along with some others, he went out in a boat and they fished all night but caught nothing. What a long, discouraging night that must have been! As they came in toward shore, early in the morning before the sun had risen, they saw someone standing on the beach, but they didn't recognize Him.

The man on shore called out, "Boys, did you catch anything?"

That voice—so familiar and yet . . .

"No," the men in the boat answered.

"Why don't you cast your nets on the other side of the boat?"

They looked at each other and thought, *Well, what harm could it do?* So they threw out the nets one last time, and suddenly it was as though every fish in the Sea of Galilee had crowded into their nets. The nets were so full that they couldn't even pull them into the boat, so they hauled all those fish to the shore.

The Bible tells us that another surprise awaited them:

> As soon as they had come to land, they saw a fire of coals there, and fish laid on it, and bread. Jesus said to them, "Bring some of the fish which you have just caught."
>
> Simon Peter went up and dragged the net to land, full of large fish, one hundred and fifty-three; and although there were so many, the net was not broken. Jesus said to them, "Come and eat breakfast." Yet none of the disciples dared ask Him, "Who are You?" — knowing that it was the Lord. Jesus then came and took the bread and gave it to them, and likewise the fish.
>
> This is now the third time Jesus showed Himself to His disciples after He was raised from the dead. (John 21:9-14)

Let's note a few things about this resurrection appearance of Jesus. John 21:4 says that "Jesus stood on the shore." He wasn't a phantom floating around. Notice also that He spoke to them with a human voice, saying, "Fellows, have you caught any fish?" (verse 5, NLT). He cooked the men some fish, broiling them over the coals. He was a real person! Later, we read that He breathed the Holy Spirit on them.

What's the point here? Just this: In our glorified bodies, you and I will be like this because those future bodies will resemble His resurrection body.

Three things in particular stand out about the glorified,

resurrected body of Christ. First, He was recognizable. The disciples recognized Him and knew Him. He would even show them the physical scars He received from the crucifixion. Second, He didn't appear to have normal limitations. He was able to appear and disappear at will, even appearing inside a closed and locked room (see John 20:19). Finally, He ate food.

What do these things say to us about our future bodies?

First, we will be recognizable. As I said, you will be you. But you also will be in a body that won't have many of the natural limitations your body has now. The blueprints for our glorified bodies are in the bodies we now possess. The fact that Christ could appear in a room and disappear without using a door is pretty fascinating, but, at the same time, you could reach out and touch Him.

What's more, our bodies will no longer age, become sick, or break down. In 1 Corinthians 15, Paul wrote, "Our earthly bodies are planted in the ground when we die, but they will be raised to live forever. Our bodies are buried in brokenness, but they will be raised in glory. They are buried in weakness, but they will be raised in strength" (verses 42-43, NLT).

I'm also happy to tell you that we will eat in our new resurrection body. When the Lord rose again from the dead, He took the opportunity to prove that point and ate a piece of fish in front of them. (An excellent menu choice, by the way.)

His disciples must have looked at each other and said, "Yes, this is our Jesus." We get the idea in the Gospels that Jesus liked to eat and was eating all the time with His disciples. In fact, in Revelation 3:20, He used eating as a metaphor of how He longed to have a relationship with us. Remember the verse?

> Here I am! I stand at the door and knock. If anyone hears my voice and opens the door, I will come in and eat with him, and he with me. (NIV)

In Revelation 19:9, we're told, "Blessed are those who are called to the marriage supper of the Lamb!" I like the word *supper.* That is what they call dinner in the south: "Y'all comin' to supper? Wash up for supper."

It reminds of when I was a kid, growing up at my grandparents' place in Arkansas. When my grandmother cooked, she would make everything from scratch. My grandfather literally would kill the chicken we'd have for dinner. He would take a chicken, put it on the block, and, *whack*, chop off its head. I remember being traumatized by the blood spurting out and the headless chicken running around like . . . a headless chicken. But you have never tasted anything like Mama Stella's fried chicken, with all the southern fixin's, like black-eyed peas, collard greens, and mashed potatoes. Her crowning achievement, however, was her biscuits. They were unbelievable, and in all the years since, I don't think I've ever tasted a biscuit that even comes close. I think at that great supper in heaven, the Lord might put Mama Stella to work up there, making biscuits that were already heavenly here on earth.

Can you imagine a feast like this—sitting around with those great men and women of the Bible and from history?

"Moses, could you pass the manna, please?"

"Excuse me, Elijah, but this meat is a little undercooked. Could you get a little fire on that for me?"

"Pardon me, Lot, but could you please pass the salt? What? Oh, goodness, Lot, you are SO sensitive!"

"Hey, that's a great question. Let's ask C. S. Lewis."

"Spurgeon, why don't you chime in on this discussion?"

"Corrie ten Boom, I loved what you always had to say on this topic."

"President Lincoln, what do you think about this?"

We will have the most amazing conversations. But heaven won't only be gathering together with the great men and women of God; heaven also will be a place of resurrected relationships. You will be reunited with your loved ones who believed in Jesus and went on before you.

Perhaps you lost a loved one unexpectedly. Communication with him or her was suddenly cut off and you long to reconnect. You ache to finish that conversation and to have new ones. In heaven, that all will be sorted out and there will be no such thing as a dropped call.

When could we begin to experience such things?

Any minute!

"CAUGHT UP"

> Since we believe that Jesus died and was raised to life again, we also believe that when Jesus returns, God will bring back with him the believers who have died.
>
> We tell you this directly from the Lord: We who are still living when the Lord returns will not meet him ahead of those who have died. For the Lord himself will come down from heaven with a commanding shout, with the voice of the archangel, and with the trumpet call of God. First, the Christians who have died will rise from their graves. Then, together with them, we who are still alive and remain on the earth will be caught up in the clouds to meet the Lord in the air. Then we will be with the Lord forever. So encourage each other with these words. (1 Thessalonians 4:14-18, NLT)

You will be going about your business in the course of a day or perhaps deep into sleep one night and will suddenly find yourself in the clouds, reunited with loved ones, and face-to-face with Jesus in your new, glorified body. And this could happen in a nanosecond. As the Bible says in 1 Corinthians, it will take place "in a flash, in the twinkling of an eye" (15:52, NIV).

The term *twinkling* comes from the Greek word *atomos*, from which we get our word *atom*. It is speaking of a time interval that is so brief that it can't be measured.

Death is the great separator; Jesus Christ is the Great Reconciler. In that wonderful moment, we will be reunited with loved ones: husbands with wives, children with parents, friends with friends. It will be like the biggest family reunion that ever was, only this one will happen "in the clouds."

You might not be too excited about the idea of a family reunion because it hasn't always been so great with your family here on earth. I understand. We all have weird family members, and we all came from dysfunctional families. In heaven, however, all the dysfunction will be gone, along with the weirdness, problems, old misunderstandings, and drama. This will be a perfect reunion as we are joined with our Lord in the air.

SO HOW SHOULD THIS AFFECT US?

If I truly believe that Jesus could return for His own at any moment, it should certainly impact the way I live, the choices I make, what I think about, what I spend my time doing, and what I spend my money on. In short, it should affect every aspect of my life.

Let me come back to a verse I quoted earlier, but this time, I'll include a couple of verses that precede it to give some context:

> Behold what manner of love the Father has bestowed on us, that we should be called children of God! Therefore the world does not know us, because it did not know Him. Beloved, now we are children of God; and it has not yet been revealed what we shall be, but we know that when He is revealed, we shall be like Him, for we shall see Him as He is. And everyone who has this hope in Him purifies himself, just as He is pure. (I John 3:1-3)

If I have the hope of the Lord's return—the "blessed hope" (Titus 2:13)—burning brightly in my conscious thoughts, it should affect the way I live. It should cause me to want to live a godly life in recognition of the fact that God loves me, has chosen me, and has so much waiting for me in heaven. How do I respond to the knowledge of our Lord's "any moment" return? I should purify myself. In other words, gratitude leads to godliness. The hopeful Christian seeks to be a holy Christian and seeks to purify his or her life from all known sin.

Here's a question for you to consider: Are there activities in your life that you would be ashamed to be doing if Christ were to return? Is there a relationship you are engaged in right now that is dragging you down spiritually? This is where the words *purify yourself* come in. To purify myself means that I make some careful decisions about what I do and what I refuse to do. It also means that I live my life with a sense of anticipation and readiness.

In so many parables that Jesus gave, He told us to be

watching and waiting and alert as we look for the return of Christ again. You will purify yourself even as He is pure.

If you find yourself longing for heaven and looking forward to the coming of Jesus for His own, that would indicate to me that your life is right with God. If, on the other hand, you never even consider heaven or don't give a passing thought to the coming of Jesus, that may indicate that your heart has drifted away from God and you need to turn from what you're doing and run back to Him as fast as you can.

If you do, you'll find that He's been waiting for you.

The porch light will be on, and the door will be open.

So will His waiting arms.

NOTES

Chapter 1: Hope for Those Facing Crisis

1. Randy Alcorn, *If God Is Good: Faith in the Midst of Suffering and Evil* (Colorado Springs, CO: Multnomah, 2009), 60.
2. C. S. Lewis, *The Problem of Pain* (New York: HarperCollins, 1996), 93–94.
3. Alcorn, 12.
4. C. S. Lewis, *The Complete C. S. Lewis Signature Classics* (New York: HarperCollins, 2002), 452.

Chapter 3: Hope for Lonely Hearts

1. Timothy Keller, *The Meaning of Marriage: Facing the Complexities of Commitment with the Wisdom of God* (New York: Dutton, 2011), 25–26.

Chapter 4: Hope for Hurting Marriages, Part I

1. Gigi Levangie Grazer, "Wasbands and Wives, Seven Reasons to Stay Married," *The Huffington Post,*

September 7, 2011, http://www.huffingtonpost.com/gigi-levangie-grazer/wasbands-and-wives-seven-_b_967170.html.

2. C. S. Lewis, *The Complete C. S. Lewis Signature Classics* (New York: HarperCollins, 2002), 94.

Chapter 5: Hope for Hurting Marriages, Part 2

1. Ed Wheat and Gloria Okes Perkins, *Love Life for Every Married Couple: How to Fall in Love and Stay in Love* (Grand Rapids, MI: Zondervan, 1997), 152–153.

Chapter 7: Hope of Heaven

1. Brian Lowery and Craig Brian Larson, *1001 Quotations That Connect: Timeless Wisdom for Teaching, Preaching, and Writing* (Grand Rapids, MI: Zondervan, 1997), 295.
2. Randy Alcorn, *We Shall See God: Charles Spurgeon's Classic Devotional Thoughts on Heaven* (Carol Stream, IL: Tyndale, 2011), 44.
3. C. S. Lewis, *The Complete C. S. Lewis Signature Classics* (New York: HarperCollins, 2002), 640.

Other Books by Greg Laurie

As I See It
Better Than Happiness
Daily Hope for Hurting Hearts
Dealing with Giants
Deepening Your Faith
Discipleship
Essentials
For Every Season, volumes 1, 2, and 3
God's Design for Christian Dating
The Great Compromise
The Greatest Stories Ever Told, volumes 1, 2, and 3
His Christmas Presence
Hope for America
Hope for Hurting Hearts
How to Know God
I'm Going on a Diet Tomorrow
Living Out Your Faith
Making God Known
Married. Happily.
Run to Win
Secrets to Spiritual Success
Signs of the Times
Start! To Follow
Strengthening Your Faith
Ten Things You Should Know About God and Life
Upside Down Living
What Every Christian Needs to Know
Why, God?
Worldview